# WORLD ENGLISH 3

**SECOND EDITION**

Real People • Real Places • Real Language

Kristin L. Johannsen and Rebecca Tarver Chase, Authors

Rob Jenkins, Series Editor

NATIONAL GEOGRAPHIC LEARNING | CENGAGE Learning®

Australia • Brazil • Japan • Korea • Mexico • Singapore • Spain • United Kingdom • United States

**World English Level 3**
Real People, Real Places, Real Language
Kristin L. Johannsen, Author
Rebecca Tarver Chase, Author
Rob Jenkins, Series Editor

Publisher: Sherrise Roehr

Executive Editor: Sarah Kenney

Senior Development Editor: Margarita Matte

Development Editor: Brenden Layte

Assistant Editor: Alison Bruno

Editorial Assistant: Patricia Giunta

Media Researcher: Leila Hishmeh

Senior Technology Product Manager: Scott Rule

Director of Global Marketing: Ian Martin

Senior Product Marketing Manager:
    Caitlin Thomas

Sr. Director, ELT & World Languages:
    Michael Burggren

Production Manager: Daisy Sosa

Content Project Manager: Andrea Bobotas

Senior Print Buyer: Mary Beth Hennebury

Cover Designer: Aaron Opie

Art Director: Scott Baker

Creative Director: Chris Roy

Cover Image: © Manuel Higuera

Compositor: MPS Limited

**Cover Image**

Moroccan market: A quiet day at
a souq in Morocco

> For product information and technology assistance, contact us at
> **Cengage Learning Customer & Sales Support, 1-800-354-9706**
>
> For permission to use material from this text or product,
> submit all requests online at **cengage.com/permissions**
> Further permissions questions can be emailed to
> **permissionrequest@cengage.com**

World English 3 ISBN: 978-1-285-84871-6
World English 3 + CD-ROM ISBN: 978-1-285-84837-2
World English 3 + Online Workbook ISBN: 978-1-305-08952-5

**National Geographic Learning**
20 Channel Center Street
Boston, MA 02210
USA

Cengage Learning is a leading provider of customized learning solutions with office locations around the globe, including Singapore, the United Kingdom, Austrailia, Mexico, Brazil, and Japan.

Cengage Learning products are represented in Canada by Nelson Education, Ltd.

Visit National Geographic Learning online at ngl.cengage.com

Visit our corporate website at www.cengage.com

Printed in the United States of America
Print Number: 05  Print Year: 2017

Thank you to the educators who provided invaluable feedback during the development of the second edition of the *World English* series:

## AMERICAS

### Brazil

**Renata Cardoso,** Universidade de Brasília, Brasília
**Gladys De Sousa,** Universidade Federal de Minas Gerais, Belo Horizonte
**Marilena Fernandes,** Associação Alumni, São Paulo
**Mary Ruth Popov,** Ingles Express, Ltda., Belo Horizonte
**Ana Rosa,** Speed, Vila Velha
**Danny Sheps,** English4u2, Natal
**Renata Zainotte,** Go Up Idiomas, Rio de Janeiro

### Colombia

**Eida Caicedo,** Universidad de San Buenaventura Cali, Cali
**Andres Felipe Echeverri Patiño,** Corporación Universitaria Lasallista, Envigado
**Luz Libia Rey,** Centro Colombo Americano, Bogota

### Dominican Republic

**Aida Rosales,** Instituto Cultural Dominico-Americano, Santo Domingo

### Ecuador

**Elizabeth Ortiz,** COPEI-Copol English Institute, Guayaquil

### Mexico

**Ramon Aguilar,** LEC Languages and Education Consulting, Hermosillo
**Claudia García-Moreno Ávila,** Universidad Autónoma del Estado de México, Toluca
**Ana María Benton,** Universidad Anahuac Mexico Norte, Huixquilucan
**Martha Del Angel,** Tecnológico de Monterrey, Monterrey
**Sachenka García B.,** Universidad Kino, Hermosillo
**Cinthia I. Navarrete García,** Universidad Autónoma del Estado de México, Toluca
**Alonso Gaxiola,** Universidad Autonoma de Sinaloa, Guasave
**Raquel Hernandez,** Tecnológico de Monterrey, Monterrey
**Beatriz Cuenca Hernández,** Universidad Autónoma del Estado de México, Toluca
**Luz María Lara Hernández,** Universidad Autónoma del Estado de México, Toluca
**Esthela Ramírez Hernández,** Universidad Autónoma del Estado de México, Toluca
**Ma Guadalupe Peña Huerta,** Universidad Autónoma del Estado de México, Toluca
**Elsa Iruegas,** Prepa Tec Campus Cumbres, Monterrey
**María del Carmen Turral Maya,** Universidad Autónoma del Estado de México, Toluca
**Lima Melani Ayala Olvera,** Universidad Autónoma del Estado de México, Toluca
**Suraya Ordorica Reyes,** Universidad Autónoma del Estado de México, Toluca
**Leonor Rosales,** Tecnológico de Monterrey, Monterrey
**Leticia Adelina Ruiz Guerrero,** ITESO, Jesuit University, Tlaquepaque

### United States

**Nancy Alaks,** College of DuPage, Glen Ellyn, IL
**Annette Barker,** College of DuPage, Aurora, IL
**Joyce Gatto,** College of Lake County, Grayslake, IL
**Donna Glade-Tau,** Harper College, Palatine, IL
**Mary "Katie" Hu,** Lone Star College – North Harris, Houston, TX
**Christy Naghitorabi,** University of South Florida, St. Petersburg, FL

## ASIA

**Beri Ali,** Cleverlearn (American Academy), Ho Chi Minh City
**Ronald Anderson,** Chonnam National University, Yeosu Campus, Jeollanam
**Michael Brown,** Canadian Secondary Wenzhou No. 22 School, Wenzhou
**Leyi Cao,** Macau University of Science and Technology, Macau
**Maneerat Chuaychoowong,** Mae Fah Luang University, Chiang Rai
**Sooah Chung,** Hwarang Elementary School, Seoul
**Edgar Du,** Vanung University, Taoyuan County
**David Fairweather,** Asahikawa Daigaku, Asahikawa
**Andrew Garth,** Chonnam National University, Yeosu Campus, Jeollanam
**Brian Gaynor,** Muroran Institute of Technology, Muroran-shi
**Emma Gould,** Chonnam National University, Yeosu Campus, Jeollanam
**David Grant,** Kochi National College of Technology, Nankoku
**Michael Halloran,** Chonnam National University, Yeosu Campus, Jeollanam
**Nina Ainun Hamdan,** University Malaysia, Kuala Lumpur
**Richard Hatcher,** Chonnam National University, Yeosu Campus, Jeollanam
**Edward Tze-Lu Ho,** Chihlee Institute of Technology, New Taipei City
**Soontae Hong,** Yonsei University, Seoul
**Chaiyathip Katsura,** Mae Fah Luang University, Chiang Rai
**Byoug-Kyo Lee,** Yonsei University, Seoul
**Han Li,** Aceleader International Language Center, Beijing
**Michael McGuire,** Kansai Gaidai University, Osaka
**Yu Jin Ng,** Universiti Tenaga Nasional, Kajang, Selangor
**Somaly Pan,** Royal University of Phnom Penh, Phnom Penh
**HyunSuk Park,** Halla University, Wonju
**Bunroeun Pich,** Build Bright University, Phnom Penh
**Renee Sawazaki,** Surugadai University, Annaka-shi
**Adam Schofield,** Cleverlearn (American Academy), Ho Chi Minh City
**Pawadee Srisang,** Burapha University, Chanthaburi Campus, Ta-Mai District
**Douglas Sweetlove,** Kinjo Gakuin University, Nagoya
**Tari Lee Sykes,** National Taiwan University of Science and Technology, Taipei
**Monika Szirmai,** Hiroshima International University, Hiroshima
**Sherry Wen,** Yan Ping High School, Taipei
**Chris Wilson,** Okinawa University, Naha City, Okinawa
**Christopher Wood,** Meijo University, Nagoya
**Evelyn Wu,** Minghsin University of Science and Technology, Xinfeng, Hsinchu County
**Aroma Xiang,** Macau University of Science and Technology, Macau
**Zoe Xie,** Macau University of Science and Technology, Macau
**Juan Xu,** Macau University of Science and Technology, Macau
**Florence Yap,** Chang Gung University, Taoyuan
**Sukanda Yatprom,** Mae Fah Luang University, Chiang Rai
**Echo Yu,** Macau University of Science and Technology, Macau

The publisher would like to extend a special thank you to Raúl Billini, English Coordinator, Mi Colegio, the Dominican Republic, for his contributions to the series.

## BACKGROUND – LEARNING AND INSTRUCTION

Learning has been described as acquiring knowledge. Obtaining knowledge does not guarantee understanding, however. A math student, for example, could replicate any number of algebraic formulas, but never come to an *understanding* of how they could be used or for what purpose he or she has learned them. If understanding is defined as the ability to use knowledge, then learning could be defined differently and more accurately. The ability of the student to use knowledge instead of merely receiving information therefore becomes the goal and the standard by which learning is assessed.

This revelation has led to classrooms that are no longer teacher-centric or lecture driven. Instead, students are asked to think, ponder, and make decisions based on the information received or, even more productive, students are asked to construct learning or discover information in personal pursuits, or with help from an instructor, with partners, or in groups. The practice they get from such approaches stimulates learning with a purpose. The purpose becomes a tangible goal or objective that provides opportunities for students to transfer skills and experiences to future learning.

In the context of language development, this approach becomes essential to real learning and understanding. Learning a language is a skill that is developed only after significant practice. Students can learn the mechanics of a language but when confronted with real-world situations, they are not capable of communication. Therefore, it might be better to shift the discussion from "Language Learning" to "Communication Building." Communication should not be limited to only the productive skills. Reading and listening serve important avenues for communication as well.

## FOUR PRINCIPLES TO DEVELOPING LEARNING ENVIRONMENTS

**Mission:** The goal or mission of a language course might adequately be stated as the pursuit of providing sufficient information and practice to allow students to communicate accurately and effectively to a reasonable extent given the level, student experiences, and time on task provided. This goal can be reflected in potential student learning outcomes identified by what students will be able to do through performance indicators.

*World English* provides a clear chart within the table of contents to show the expected outcomes of the course. The books are designed to capture student imagination and allow students ample opportunities to communicate. A study of the table of contents identifies the process of communication building that will go on during the course.

**Context:** It is important to identify what vehicle will be used to provide instruction. If students are to learn through practice, language cannot be introduced as isolated verb forms, nouns, and modifiers. It must have context. To reach the learners and to provide opportunities to communicate, the context must be interesting and relevant to learners' lives and expectations. In other words, there must be a purpose and students must have a clear understanding of what that purpose is.

*World English* provides a meaningful context that allows students to connect with the world. Research has demonstrated pictures and illustrations are best suited for creating interest and motivation within learners. National Geographic has a long history of providing magnificent learning environments through pictures, illustrations, true accounts, and video. The pictures, stories, and video capture the learners' imagination and "hook" them to learning in such a way that students have significant reasons to communicate promoting interaction and critical thinking. The context will also present students with a desire to know more, leading to life-long learning.

## Objectives (Goals)

With the understanding that a purpose for communicating is essential, identifying precisely what the purpose is in each instance becomes crucial even before specifics of instruction have been defined. This is often called "backward design." Backward design means, in the context of classroom lesson planning, that first desired outcomes, goals, or objectives are defined and then lessons are mapped out with the end in mind, the end being what students will be able to do after sufficient instruction and practice. Having well-crafted objectives or goals provides the standard by which learners' performance can be assessed or self-assessed.

*World English* lessons are designed on two-page spreads so students can easily see what is expected and what the context is. The goal that directly relates to the final application activity is identified at the beginning. Students, as well as instructors, can easily evaluate their performance as they attempt the final activity. Students can also readily see what tools they will practice to prepare them for the application activity. The application activity is a task where students can demonstrate their ability to perform what the lesson goal requires. This information provides direction and purpose for the learner. Students, who know what is expected, where they are going, and how they will get there, are more apt to reach success. Each success builds confidence and additional communication skills.

## Tools and Skills

Once the lesson objective has been identified and a context established, the lesson developer must choose the tools the learner will need to successfully perform the task or objective. The developer can choose among various areas in communication building including vocabulary, grammar and pronunciation. The developer must also choose skills and strategies including reading, writing, listening, and speaking. The receptive skills of reading and listening are essential components to communication. All of these tools and skills must be placed in a balanced way into a context providing practice that can be transferred to their final application or learner demonstration which ultimately becomes evidence of communication building.

*World English* units are divided into "lessons" that each consists of a two-page spread. Each spread focuses on different skills and strategies and is labeled by a letter (A-E). The units contain the following lesson sequence:

A: Vocabulary
B: Listening and Pronunciation
C: Language Expansion
D: Reading/Writing
E: Video Journal

Additional grammar and vocabulary are introduced as tools throughout to provide practice for the final application activity. Each activity in a page spread has the purpose of developing adequate skills to perform the final application task.

## LAST WORD

The philosophy of *World English* is to provide motivating content to connect students to the world through which they build communication skills. These skills are developed, practiced, and assessed from lesson to lesson through initially identifying the objective and giving learners the tools they need to complete a final application task. The concept of performance is highlighted over merely learning new information and performance comes from communicating about meaningful and useful context. An accumulation of small communication skills leads to true and effective communication outside of the classroom in real-world environments.

Rob Jenkins, Series Editor

| | | Unit Goals | Grammar | Vocabulary |
|---|---|---|---|---|
| **UNIT 1** | **People and Places** Page 2 | • Discuss reasons for living where you do<br>• Explain why you plan stay or leave<br>• Describe a new place<br>• Describe the city where you live | Present perfect tense vs. present continuous tense<br>***She has moved*** *three times in her life.*<br>***It's been raining*** *all day.*<br>*So + adjective + that*<br>*It's **so** dry here **that** water is brought in on trucks.* | Migration<br>Climate |
| **UNIT 2** | **The Mind** Page 14 | • Talk about learning strategies<br>• Talk about your senses<br>• Talk about your fears<br>• Describe an emotional experience | Gerunds as subjects and after prepositions<br>***Learning*** *English is important.*<br>*We talked about **studying** together.*<br>*May, might,* and *could* for possibility<br>*We **may** find dangerous animals in the jungle.* | Thought processes<br>Scientific studies |
| **UNIT 3** | **Changing Planet** Page 26 | • Suggest solutions to environmental problems<br>• Discuss causes and effects<br>• Talk about invasive species<br>• Discuss effects on the future | The passive—all tenses<br>*Often, trees **are removed** to make room for farming.*<br>The past perfect<br>*By the time sea level **had risen** ten feet…* | Environmental changes<br>Large numbers |

**TED**TALKS Video Page 38 **Paul Nicklen: Tales of Ice-bound Wonderlands**

| | | Unit Goals | Grammar | Vocabulary |
|---|---|---|---|---|
| **UNIT 4** | **Money vs. Wealth** Page 42 | • Describe your financial habits<br>• Discuss things that people value<br>• Talk about banking<br>• Talk about different types of wealth | Gerund vs. infinitive<br>*I **try to make** a budget. / I **enjoy finding** bargains.*<br>Review of the passive voice<br>*Coffee **is grown** in Brazil.*<br>*That movie **was made** by two teenagers.* | Money transactions<br>Banking |
| **UNIT 5** | **Survival** Page 54 | • Talk about emergency situations<br>• Evaluate survival methods<br>• Describe how animals survive<br>• Write a Brochure | Unreal conditional in the present<br>*If they **weren't** inside the shelter, they **would** quickly **die**.*<br>*Wish* in the present<br>*I **wish** I had **brought** a good book to read in the shelter.* | Survival skills<br>Environmental conservation |
| **UNIT 6** | **Art** Page 66 | • Report what another person said<br>• Express your opinions about a piece of art<br>• Describe your favorite artists and their art<br>• Talk about public art | Reported speech<br>***She said she was tired and her head hurt.***<br>Subject adjective clauses<br>*An artist **who works with clay has strong hands.*** | Art<br>Art materials |

**TED**TALKS Video Page 78 **Amit Sood: Building a Museum of Museums on the Web**

| Listening | Speaking and Pronunciation | Reading | Writing | Video Journal |
|---|---|---|---|---|
| Focused listening<br><br>Interviews about why people live where they do | Discussing reasons for staying or moving<br><br>Contractions with *have* and *be* | **National Geographic:**<br>"Pioneers of the Pacific" | Writing a paragraph about a city | **National Geographic:**<br>"San Francisco's Mission District" |
| Listening for general understanding and specific information<br><br>A radio program about the unusual condition of synesthesia | Talking about sensations<br><br>*Th* sounds | **National Geographic:**<br>"In Your Face" | Writing about a personal experience | **National Geographic:**<br>"Memory Man" |
| General and focused listening<br><br>Climate change | Discussing cause and effect<br><br>Linking words together | **TED**TALKS<br>"Salvation (and Profit) in Greentech" | Writing a news article | **National Geographic:**<br>"The Netherlands: Rising Water" |
| General and focused listening<br><br>Radio program:<br>  The history of money | Giving suggestions for how to have fun for free<br><br>Reduction of *to* | **TED**TALKS<br>"Music is Medicine, Music is Sanity" | Writing a paragraph about valued things | **National Geographic:**<br>"Making a Deal" |
| Listening for general understanding<br><br>A radio program interviewing survivors | Simulation:<br>  working with a team in a survival situation<br><br>Reduced sounds:<br>  *d'ya* and *didja* | **National Geographic:**<br>"Survival School" | Writing an advertising brochure | **National Geographic:**<br>"Andean Weavers" |
| Listening for general understanding<br><br>Conversations in a museum | Discussing personal selections<br><br>Thought groups | **National Geographic:**<br>"Saving a City's Public Art" | Writing a detailed description | **National Geographic:**<br>"Faces of India" |

| | Unit Goals | Grammar | Vocabulary |
|---|---|---|---|
| **UNIT 7** Getting Around  Page 82 | • Talk about new developments<br>• Discuss choices in transportation<br>• Use English to get around<br>• Make recommendations for improving transportation | Passive voice with the present continuous and present perfect tenses<br>*The new **plane is being tested** now. /Computers **have been used** for more than 50 years.*<br>Indirect questions<br>*Do you know **if the bus stops** here?* | Modern transportation<br>Public transportation |
| **UNIT 8** Competition  Page 94 | • Talk about sports<br>• Explain which sport is best for you<br>• Talk about positive and negative aspects of competition<br>• Discuss competitive advantages | Negative questions<br>***Don't** you want to go downtown with us?*<br>Adjective clauses with object pronouns<br>*The medal **that he won** was made of gold.* | Sportsmanship<br>Sports |
| **UNIT 9** Danger  Page 106 | • Discuss ways to stay safe<br>• Talk about dangerous work<br>• Discuss personal emergencies<br>• Discuss dangerous situations | Tag questions<br>*Those spiders are poisonous, **aren't they?***<br>Adverbial clauses of time<br>*I finished my project **before** I went home.* | Dangerous things<br>Expressions for emergencies |

**TED**TALKS  Video  Page 118  **Mark Bezos: A Life Lesson from a Volunteer Firefighter**

| | Unit Goals | Grammar | Vocabulary |
|---|---|---|---|
| **UNIT 10** Mysteries  Page 122 | • Speculate about mysteries<br>• Discuss types of mysteries<br>• Talk about plans you used to have<br>• Explain a mysterious image | Modals for speculating about the past<br>*He **might have seen** a large fish instead of a sea monster.*<br>The future in the past<br>*The two sisters **were going** to have a picnic by the lake.* | Ancient mysteries<br>Reactions to surprise |
| **UNIT 11** Learning  Page 134 | • Talk about educational choices<br>• Discuss your learning style<br>• Talk about choosing a university major<br>• Propose a new approach to teaching | *Should have, Would have, Could have*<br>*I **should have applied** for a scholarship.*<br>Noun clauses<br>*I don't know **when the deadline is.*** | Education<br>University majors |
| **UNIT 12** Space  Page 146 | • Talk about the future<br>• Talk about life in space<br>• Speculate about the future<br>• Summarize a sequence of events | Talking about the future<br>*Space exploration **will/is going to** be even more international in the future.*<br>Modals and modal-like phrases to talk about the future<br>***We'll be able to** see it from here.* | Space exploration<br>Future time expressions |

**TED**TALKS  Video  Page 158  **Bill Stone: I'm Going to the Moon. Who's with Me?**

| Listening | Speaking and Pronunciation | Reading | Writing | Video Journal |
|---|---|---|---|---|
| Focused listening<br>A discussion:<br>  Subway systems | Role-play:<br>  solving an airport problem<br>Reduced *are* | **National Geographic:**<br>"The Rickshaws of Kolkata" | Writing a letter to the editor of a newspaper | **National Geographic:**<br>"Big City Bicycle Messengers" |
| Listening for general understanding and specific information<br>Sports interviews | Matching sports to personalities<br>Intonation to show surprise | **National Geographic:**<br>"In Sports, Red is the Winning Color" | Writing a list of competition tips | **National Geographic:**<br>"Women in The Rodeo" |
| Focused and general listening<br>Radio program:<br>  An unusual job | Role-play:<br>  a newspaper interview<br>Intonation of tag questions | **TED**TALKS<br>"Three Things I Learned While My Plane Crashed" | Writing about emergency preparations | **National Geographic:**<br>"Destroyers" |
| Listening for general understanding<br>Interview of sea monster expert | Discussing different types of mysteries<br>Intonation: Finished and unfinished ideas | **National Geographic:**<br>"Hands Across Time" | Writing a comparison | **National Geographic:**<br>"Crop Circles" |
| Listening for general understanding<br>Learning experiences | Discussing quiz results<br>Past modals | **TED**TALKS<br>"Five Dangerous Things (You Should Let Your Children Do)" | Writing about new approaches to teaching | **National Geographic:**<br>"Butler School" |
| General and focused listening<br>Interview of an astronaut | Role-play:<br>  Choosing a space experiment<br>Stress in compound nouns | **National Geographic:**<br>"The Hubble Space Telescope" | Writing about space exploration | **National Geographic:**<br>"Daring Mighty Things: Curiosity Lands on Mars" |

Reindeer herder and his flock in a
Siberian valley

**Look at the photo, answer the questions:**

1 What do you see in the picture?

2 Why do you think people live in this place?

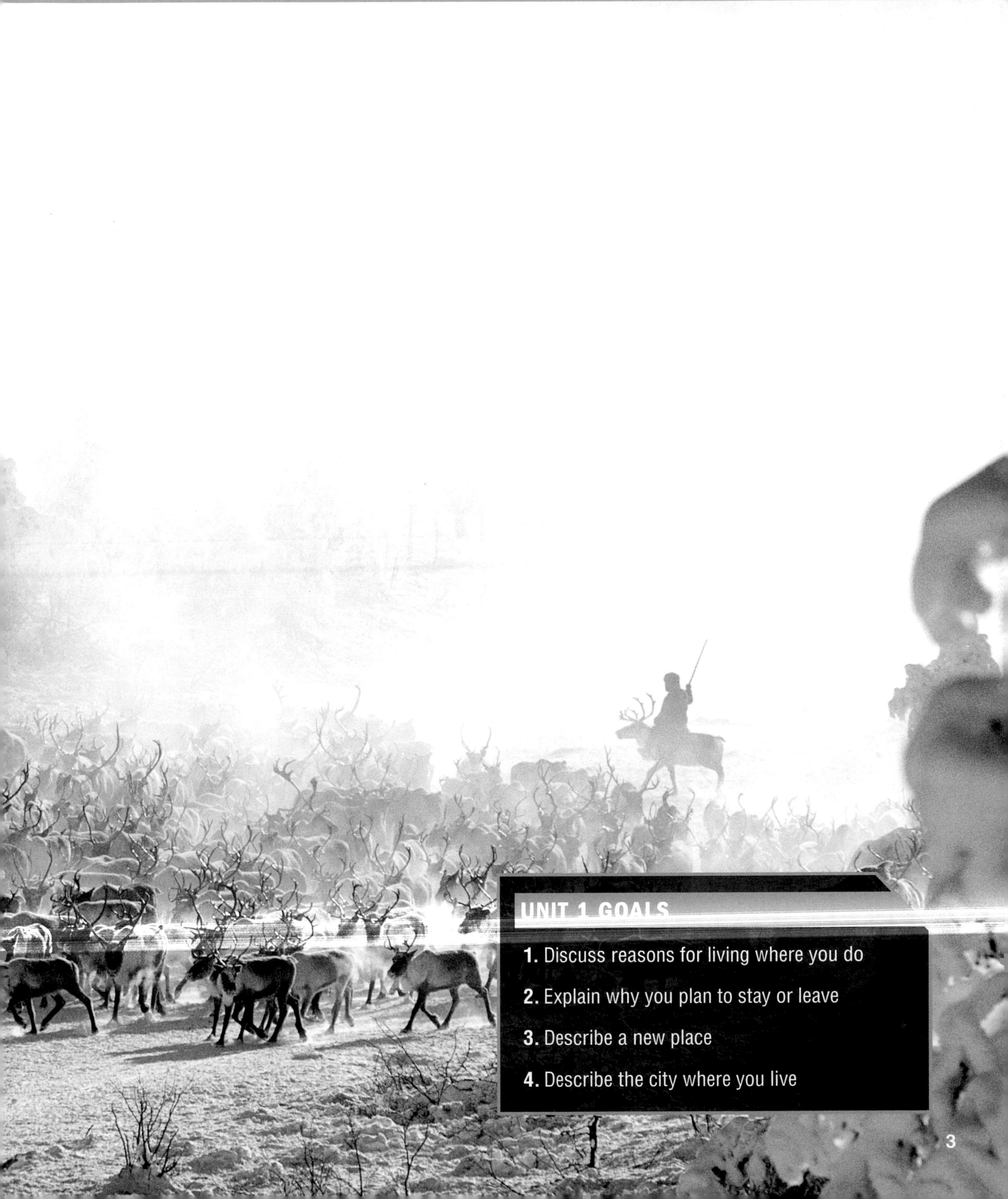

## UNIT 1 GOALS

1. Discuss reasons for living where you do
2. Explain why you plan to stay or leave
3. Describe a new place
4. Describe the city where you live

▲ Woman walking with cargo in the Andes, Peru

### Word Focus

We often use *for* and *since* with the present perfect to talk about how long a situation has lasted.

## Vocabulary

**A** Read the text and notice the words in blue.

Why do people move to new places? Long ago, ancient people wanted to inhabit places with plenty of food and other resources. These people got food in the same ways we do now: farming, hunting or herding animals, or fishing if they lived near water.

Because of competition for food, overcrowding was one reason early people moved. They sometimes walked very long distances or rode on animals, or they would sail across the ocean.

Nowadays, modern people may move in search of employment or a better climate. The migration of large groups of people may occur because of economic problems or a lack of food or water. Political problems can also cause people to migrate.

**B** Write the words in blue next to their meanings in your notebook.

1. to live in a place
2. travel in a boat
3. catching fish
4. moving from one place to another
5. killing animals for food

6. a job; work
7. very old
8. caring for animals
9. to happen
10. relating to government

## Grammar: Present perfect vs. present perfect continuous tense

| | |
|---|---|
| Form the present perfect with: Subject + *has/have* + (*not*) + past participle of a verb. | **Sean has moved** five times in his life, and he plans to move again next year. |
| Use the present perfect to talk about things that: <br> 1. began in the past and continue until now. <br> 2. have happened several times. <br> 3. happened at an unspecified past time and are connected with the present. | 1. **Professor Brown has spoken** Swahili since he was a child. <br> 2. **We've had** three big earthquakes this year, and many people have left. <br> 3. **I've** already **eaten** breakfast, so I'll just have some coffee, please. |
| Form the present perfect continuous with: Subject + *has/have* + *been* + present participle (*-ing* form) of a verb. | **Laura has been staying** with her cousins while her parents are in Europe. |
| Use the present perfect continuous to emphasize: <br> 1. that things which began in the past are unfinished or temporary. <br> 2. how long something has been in progress. | 1. **They've been trying** to improve the city's transportation system, but it's still difficult to get around. <br> 2. **It's been raining** all day. |

**A** Complete the sentences. Use the present perfect or present perfect continuous.

1. Can we go to a different movie? I _____ (see) that one already.

2. My father _____ (work) on a fishing boat his whole life.

3. So far it _____ (snow) three times this week.

4. Our teacher _____ (live) in five countries, so she's not surprised by different beliefs and customs.

5. I can't find my dictionary, so I _____ (use) my friend's this week.

6. George _____ (try) to find a better job, but he hasn't found one.

▲ Harbor in Cape Town, South Africa

## Conversation

**A** 🔊 2 Listen to the conversation. What does Sonia like about where she lives?

**Jacob:** Do you like living here?

**Sonia:** Sure. Don't you?

**Jacob:** I guess so, but I've been reading about a lot of interesting places, and I've been thinking about moving someplace else.

**Sonia:** Well, Cape Town is a pretty interesting place, too. People have lived here for a long time because it's a good place to live.

**Jacob:** Why do you say that?

**Sonia:** It's near the ocean, for one thing, so there's always fresh seafood.

**Jacob:** That's true.

**Sonia:** And the weather is usually nice. It's never very cold, and we don't get serious storms very often.

**Jacob:** OK, but is it really an interesting place?

**Sonia:** I think so. Hey, let's go to the historical museum. We can find out about some of the fascinating things that have happened here.

**B** 🔁 Practice the conversation with a partner. Make new conversations about your home town, your country's capital city, or the city you're living in now.

**C** Make a chart like the one on the right in your notebook. Write at least three reasons for each section of the chart.

**D** 🔁 **GOAL CHECK** ✔ **Discuss reasons for living where you do**

Tell a partner why you live where you live. Has your family lived there for a long time? What do you like and dislike about living there? Why?

| Why people want to live in a place |
| --- |
| |

| Why people want to move away |
| --- |
| |

**Sheep herder in Australia**

## Listening

**A** 🔁 Rank the reasons for living in a certain place (1 = most important), and add one more reason. Share your rankings with a partner.

_____ the climate

_____ one's ancestors lived there

_____ having family members nearby

_____ environmental quality (clean air, water, etc.)

_____ employment opportunities

_____ _____

**B** 🔊 3 Listen to people talk about where they live, and answer the questions.

|  | Where does the speaker live? | Why does the speaker live there? | Does the speaker plan to move? |
| --- | --- | --- | --- |
| Speaker #1 |  |  |  |
| Speaker #2 |  |  |  |
| Speaker #3 |  |  |  |
| Speaker #4 |  |  |  |

**C** 🔊 3 Listen again. Do the speakers mention any of the reasons from exercise **A**? Which ones?

## Pronunciation: Contractions with *have* and *be*

**A** 🔊 4  English speakers often use contractions with auxiliary verbs. Listen to the pronunciation of *have* and *has*. Listen again and repeat the sentences.

| | |
|---|---|
| I have never been to Africa. | I've never been to Africa. |
| Ron has gone there twice. | Ron's gone there twice. |

**B** 🔊 5  Listen to the full and contracted forms of *be*. Listen again and repeat the sentences.

| | |
|---|---|
| Tanya is moving to Singapore. | Tanya's moving to Singapore. |
| We are paid twice a month. | We're paid twice a month. |

**C** 🔄  Work with a partner. Change the full forms of *have* and *be* to contractions, and then practice saying the sentences.

1. We have been living in Beijing for seven years.
2. Marsha is planning to visit us in December.
3. I am going to give her a call tonight.
4. They have never stayed in the same place for more than two years.
5. We are taking the train from Nairobi to Mombasa.
6. I have always wanted to go there.

▲ Park in Autumn, Sapporo, Japan

**Real Language**

To *give someone a call* means to call someone on the telephone

## Communication

**A** 🔄  Interview your partner and take notes on his or her answers.

| | |
|---|---|
| Why do you live where you live? | |
| How are your reasons different from your parents' or grandparents' reasons? | |
| What might make you want to move to a new place? | |

**B** 👥  Join another pair of students. Tell the group what you learned about your partner.

**C** 👥  **GOAL CHECK** ✓  **Explain why you plan to stay or leave**

In a small group, find out how many people plan to move someday. Ask those people to explain why they want to go to a new place. Ask the people who don't want to move to give their reasons for staying.

▲ A hot, dry day in Ghana, Africa

## Language Expansion: Climate

**A** Match the adjectives with the places they describe. Use your dictionary to help you.

**tropical**            places that receive very little rain

**temperate**          places that receive a large amount of rain

**snowy**              places with distinct seasons that are
                      never extremely hot or cold

**rainy**              places that receive a large amount of snow

**arid**               extremely cold places

**frigid**             hot, humid places near Earth's equator

**B** With a partner, fill in the blanks with places on Earth that fit the descriptions.

1. _____ has a tropical climate.
2. _____ has a temperate climate.
3. _____ has a snowy climate.

4. _____ has a rainy climate.
5. _____ has an arid climate.
6. _____ has a frigid climate.

## Grammar: *So* + adjective + *that*

Use *so* + adjective + *that* to explain that:
(1) a condition is quite extreme and (2) that it has a result.

| Condition | Result |
|---|---|
| He was **so** tired | **that** he fell asleep when his head touched the pillow. |
| The climate is **so** dry here | **that** water is brought in on trucks. |

**A** Complete the conversation. Use *so* + adjective + *that*.

**Mia:** How was your trip to Ghana?

**Daniel:** Great! But Ghana has a tropical climate, so it's hot all the time.

**Mia:** Really? How hot was it when you were there?

**Daniel:** It was (1) _____ I didn't mind taking cold showers every day. It also rained a lot while I was there.

**Mia:** How rainy was it?

**Daniel:** It was (2) _____ I carried my umbrella everywhere I went. The people in Ghana were very friendly, though, so I didn't mind the weather.

**Mia:** That's good. How friendly were they?

**Daniel:** Many of them were (3) _____ they invited me to their homes for dinner right after they met me. I ate some wonderful home-cooked meals!

**B** Complete the sentences with any appropriate adjective.

1. Yesterday, I was very _____ .

2. In January, my country is very _____ .

3. Before an important test, most students are very

   _____ .

4. The climate in Antarctica is very _____ .

5. Someday, I will be very _____ .

**C** 🔁 Take turns. Say a sentence from exercise **B.** Then ask
questions using *how* and answer them with *so* + adjective + *that*.

## Conversation

**A** 🔊 **6** Listen to the telephone conversation. How has Ryan's life changed
recently?

**Sandra:** How's it going, Ryan? Are you getting used to your new home?

**Ryan:** I'm all right. It's a very big city, though, so it takes forever to get
anyplace.

**Sandra:** Really? What about the new subway system? Isn't it fast?

**Ryan:** The trains are fast, but they're so crowded that sometimes you
have to wait for the next one. I can take buses, of course, but they
make a lot of stops.

**Sandra:** I see what you mean.

**Ryan:** Fortunately, I love my new job, and it's right downtown.

**Sandra:** That's nice! You can walk around on your lunch hour.

**Ryan:** That's exactly what I've been doing! I've been looking for good
restaurants.

**Sandra:** That's great! You know I like trying new restaurants.

**Ryan:** That's right. When you visit me, I'll know where to take you to eat.

**B** 🔁 Practice the conversation with a partner. Switch roles and practice it again.

**C** 🔁 Continue the conversation. Use your imagination to ask and answer
questions about the topics in the box:

- the people who live there
- Ryan's new job

**D** 🔁 **GOAL CHECK** ✓ **Describe a new place**

Imagine that you've been living in a new place for a few weeks. Where are
you? Tell a partner about your life in your new home.

▲ Walking through a penguin
colony in Antarctica

> Yesterday, I was
> very happy.

> How happy were you?

> I was so happy that I
> couldn't stop smiling.

## Reading

**A** Find answers to these questions in the reading.

1. When did the Lapita migration occur?

   _____

   _____

2. Where did the Lapita voyages begin?

   _____

   _____

3. How far into the Pacific did the Lapita people travel? _____

   _____

4. What aspect of Lapita culture came from the Philippines? _____

   _____

5. In which direction do the trade winds usually blow? _____

   _____

6. How does El Niño affect the trade winds? _____

   _____

**B** 🗘 After you read, talk to a partner about possible answers to these questions.

1. Why do you think the Lapita left their homes and sailed to Pacific Islands?

2. What might archaeologists find in a cemetery that would help them to understand an ancient culture?

3. How might the Lapita have sailed so far and located so many islands without modern technology?

South Pacific

# PIONEERS OF THE
# PACIFIC

No one is sure how they did it or even why they did it, but over 3,000 years ago people sailed into the enormous emptiness of the Pacific Ocean in simple canoes. Within a few centuries, these people—now known as the Lapita—had migrated from the volcanoes of Papua New Guinea to the island of Tonga, at least 2,000 miles to the east. They explored millions of square miles of the Pacific, and they discovered and then inhabited dozens of tropical islands never before seen by human eyes: Vanuatu, New Caledonia, Fiji, Samoa.

**Fishing in a canoe**

**voyage** *a long journey on a ship*   **cemetery** *a place where people are buried*
**sediment** *soil that has settled to the bottom*

There is much we do not know about the Lapita. Although their **voyages** began in the northern islands of Papua New Guinea, their language came from Taiwan, and their style of pottery decoration probably had its roots in the northern Philippines. So who were the Lapita? Did they come from a single point in Asia or from several different places?

Now, archaeologists Matthew Spriggs and Stuart Bedford of the Australian National University are working to answer these questions. A Lapita **cemetery** on the island of Ēfatē in the Pacific nation of Vanuatu has revealed information about Lapita customs, and DNA from the ancient bones may help to answer questions about the Lapita people. "This represents the best opportunity we've had yet," says Spriggs, "to find out who the Lapita actually were, where they came from, and who their closest descendants are today."

But even if the archaeologists can answer these questions, we still won't know how the Lapita sailed so far east against the trade winds, which normally blow from east to west. Atholl Anderson, professor of prehistory at the Australian National University, suggests that El Niño, the same warming of ocean water that affects the Pacific today, may have helped. Climate data obtained from slow-growing corals around the Pacific and from lake-bed **sediments** in the Andes of South America indicate a series of unusually frequent El Niños around the time of the Lapita expansion. By reversing the regular east-to-west flow of the trade winds for weeks at a time, these *super El Niños* might have carried the Lapita sailors on long, unplanned voyages far over the horizon.

However they arrived on the islands, the Lapita came to stay. Their descendants have inhabited the region for thousands of years, and why not? They're living in an island paradise that many of us only dream about.

A modern Hawaiian voyaging canoe built on ancient designs

# D GOAL 4: Describe the City Where You Live

Traveling on a canoe in Fiji, Melanesia, South Pacific

**climate and beauty of the city**

**cultural attractions and activities**

**employment**

**public transportation**

**quality of life**

## Communication

**A** 🔁 Imagine that the city where you live is trying to encourage more people to move there. Follow the instructions with a partner.

1. Use the topics in the box to discuss the benefits of life in your city.

2. For each topic, list two or three positive things that your city offers.

## Writing

**A** Write a paragraph about one attractive aspect of life in your city. Follow the steps.

1. Choose a topic from exercise **A** or use your own idea.

2. Write a good topic sentence to begin your paragraph. Then write supporting details that describe the good things about your city to a reader. For example, write:

*Centerburg has been a cultural center for a long time, and there are so many enjoyable cultural activities here that it is difficult to choose just one. People who want to reflect on the past, for example, can enjoy the historical museum, which has beautiful old objects from this country and from around the world. On weekends, the museum offers special classes just for children…*

### Word Focus

Use a variety of words in your writing:

| | |
|---|---|
| positive | attractive |
| good | beneficial |
| enjoyable | pleasant |

**B** 👥 **GOAL CHECK** ✓ **Describe the city where you live**

Read your paragraph aloud to a small group or to the whole class. Ask your classmates to suggest other details you could add to your paragraph.

Golden Gate Bridge,
San Francisco, U.S.A.

## Before You Watch

**A** 🗨 Discuss these questions with a partner. What do you know about San Francisco, California? What might attract immigrants to that city? What parts of their culture do immigrants bring with them?

## While You Watch

**A** ▶ Watch the video and match the people with their roles.

1. Ray Patlan _____
2. Juan Pedro Gaffney _____
3. Father Dan McGuire _____

a. mural artist
b. priest at Saint Peter's Church
c. director of Choir of San Francisco

▲ Large mural in an alley way in San Francisco, CA.

**B** ▶ Complete the video summary with words from the box.

| | |
|---|---|
| churches | arts |
| Spanish | Central |
| special | integration |

The Mission District is special in several ways. Religion has played a role in the community since the (1) _____ arrived. Today, large (2) _____, such as the Mission Dolores Basilica, are places where immigrants practice their religious traditions. Music also makes the neighborhood (3) _____. The Spanish Choir of San Francisco has performed to raise money for people after natural disasters in (4) _____ America. The visual arts also make it a special place. Balmy Alley is famous for its murals, and a local (5) _____ organization leads people on walking tours. A priest explains that the (6) _____ of different cultures makes the Mission District a beautiful place.

## After You Watch/Communication

**A** 🗨 If you lived in the Mission District, what would you enjoy about the neighborhood?

# The Mind

An Eastern screech owl in its nest

**UNIT 2 GOALS**

1. Talk about learning strategies

2. Talk about your senses

3. Talk about your fears

4. Describe an emotional experience

▲ Taxi in London, England

a. ways of doing an activity
b. learn to remember exactly
c. microscopic part of the body
d. make a picture in your mind
e. remembering
f. keep, continue to have
g. part
h. in your mind
i. respond
j. outstanding building or other feature

## Vocabulary

**A** Read the article. Match the words in blue with their meanings in the box.

### A Bigger Brain

Every day, Glen McNeill rides his motorbike around London for seven hours. He wants to become a taxi driver, so he must memorize every street in the city and then pass a test called "The Knowledge of London." He will answer questions about 400 routes between important places. It's an incredible test of memory. The examiner names two places, and candidates must react quickly and give the names of every street and landmark along the route between those two places.

Preparing for the exam takes three years, and passing it is extremely difficult. Some people try as many as twelve times. McNeill uses many different techniques for studying at home. He visualizes all the places on a route to make a mental map. He also concentrates on recalling street names that sound similar.

Now scientists have discovered important differences in these drivers' brains. The portion of the brain that retains information about places is larger in London taxi drivers than in other people. Learning "The Knowledge" might make their brains grow new cells.

1. memorize _b_
2. react ____
3. techniques ____
4. visualize ____
5. mental ____

6. landmark ____
7. portion ____
8. retain ____
9. cell ____
10. recalling ____

**B** 🔁 Discuss these questions with a partner. Do you think you would pass "The Knowledge" test? What would you do to learn all the streets of London?

## Grammar: Gerunds as subjects and after prepositions

| A gerund is a noun formed from a verb + *ing*. | ask → *asking*   sit → *sitting*   try → *trying* |
|---|---|
| Gerunds can be used as the subject of a sentence. | ***Saying*** new vocabulary words is a good way to remember them.<br>***Learning*** English is important for my future. |
| Gerunds can be used after a preposition. | I'm interested <u>in</u> **becoming** a taxi driver.<br>We talked <u>about</u> **studying** together.<br>He's afraid <u>of</u> **flying** on airplanes. |

### Engage!

What was the most difficult exam you have ever taken? How did you prepare for it?

**A** 🔄 Find five gerunds in the article about taxi drivers. Tell a partner why each one was used.

**B** Complete each sentence with the gerund form of a verb from the box.

study   do   travel   learn   forget   lose

1. He's tired of _____ for the taxi driver's exam.

2. Jackie is interested in _____ to China to learn about Chinese history.

3. I worry about _____ information from professors' lectures. What if I can't remember it when I take the exam?

4. For many people, _____ with their eyes, or visual learning, is the best way to remember things.

5. _____ something physical, like making something with one's hands, can be a good way to learn.

6. I'm afraid of _____ my wallet, so I always keep it in the same place.

**C** 🔄 Tell your partner about good ways to do these things. Use gerunds.

remember birthdays   practice listening to English   get more exercise

## Conversation

**A** 🔊 7 Listen to the conversation with your book closed. What did Diane forget?

**Katie:** Hi, Diane. You don't look very happy.

**Diane:** I'm not. I had an important business meeting this afternoon, and I completely forgot to bring my laptop. My boss was really upset.

**Katie:** Everybody forgets things sometimes. You shouldn't worry about it.

**Diane:** I have such a terrible memory!

**Katie:** Making a list is a good way of remembering things. That always helps me.

**Diane:** But I'll just forget about the list!

**Katie:** If you put it on top of your keys, you'll see it when you go out. That's what I always do.

**B** 🔄 Practice the conversation with a partner. Then make new conversations about important things you need to remember and good ways to remember them.

**C** 🔄 **GOAL CHECK** ✔ **Talk about learning strategies**

Discuss the learning strategies in the box. How could you use each strategy to remember new vocabulary or other things that you need to memorize?

Word Focus

Other common combinations of verb + preposition:

**worry about**
**look forward to**
**plan on**
**be tired of**
**think about**

Walking to school is a good way to get more exercise.

You could learn a new grammar structure by practicing it a lot.

taking notes   making lists
concentrating/paying attention
asking questions/participating
visualizing   practicing

▲ The Scream by Edvard Munch, who had synesthesia

## Listening

**A** 🗩 Discuss these questions with a partner.

1. What's your favorite song? Why do you like it?

2. When you listen to the song, does it make you think of any of these things?

**B** 🔊 8 Listen to a radio program about an unusual brain condition called *synesthesia*. Circle the answers.

1. When a person has synesthesia, two kinds of ( memories | senses ) work together.

2. Lori Blackman is unusual because she always sees ( letters | sounds ) in different colors.

| a person   a color   an experience   a place   a season   a picture |

# SYNESTHESIA

**C** 🔊 8 Listen again. Circle **T** for *true* and **F** for *false*.

1. The word *synesthesia* comes from the Greek words for *together* and *senses*.      **T**    **F**

2. There are two different kinds of synesthesia.      **T**    **F**

3. Lori's father has synesthesia, too.      **T**    **F**

4. Some artists and musicians have synesthesia.      **T**    **F**

5. Lori has a lot of problems because of synesthesia.      **T**    **F**

**D** 🔊 8 Listen again and fill in the information.

1. The most common kind is called _____ synesthesia.

2. Lori realized she was unusual when she was _____ years old.

3. For Lori, the letter B is light _____ .

4. About one person in _____ has synesthesia.

**E** 🗩 Discuss the questions with a partner.

1. Do you know someone who has had experiences like this?

2. Would you like to have synesthesia? If so, what kind? If not, why not?

## Pronunciation *Th* sounds

**A** 🔊 **9** *Th* has two pronunciations in English—voiced /ð/ and unvoiced /θ/. Listen and repeat the words, and notice the pronunciations of *th*.

| Voiced /ð/ | Unvoiced /θ/ |
|---|---|
| the | think |
| this | three |
| that | theater |

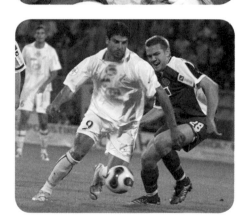

**B** 🔄 Take turns saying the words. Decide which /*th*/ sounds are voiced /ð/ and which are unvoiced /θ/.

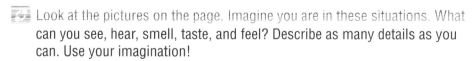

| thousand | those | Thursday | they | thank | thief | thirsty | them |

**C** Read the sentence below. Which words have voiced /ð/? Which words have unvoiced /θ/? Say the sentence out loud as fast as you can.

**I thanked that thin thief for the three theater tickets.**

## Communication

Look at the pictures on the page. Imagine you are in these situations. What can you see, hear, smell, taste, and feel? Describe as many details as you can. Use your imagination!

**B** 🔄 **GOAL CHECK** ✓ **Talk about your senses**

Work with a partner. Imagine you are in your favorite place in the world. What can you see, hear, smell, taste, touch, and feel right now?

> I feel warm sand under my feet. I smell the ocean.

Green tree python

## Language Expansion: Scientific studies

**A** Study the words in the box about science and their meanings.

laboratory—a place where scientists work

research—studying something to discover new facts

theory—a scientific idea

survey—collecting the same information from people

experiment—a scientific test to see if something is true

results—the information that scientists get after an experiment

conduct—organize and carry out

conclusion—something you decide after looking at all the information

**B** Complete the article with the correct form of a word from the box.

Everyone is afraid of snakes, right? In one (1) _____, 51 percent of people said that snakes are their biggest fear! One (2) _____ says that fear is built into our brain. But (3) _____ shows we might also learn to be afraid of things. Scientists (4) _____ an interesting (5) _____ with monkeys to find out if this is true. The monkeys were born in a (6) _____ at a university. First, they showed the monkeys videos of snakes, and the monkeys didn't react. However, when they showed videos of wild monkeys acting afraid of snakes, the lab monkeys became afraid too.

Next, a new video was shown where the wild monkeys appeared to be afraid of flowers. This time, the lab monkeys did not develop a fear of flowers. The (7) _____ of this experiment show that monkeys can learn some of their fear by watching other monkeys. The researchers' (8) _____ was that fear is partly built into monkeys' brains, but can also be learned.

**C** Discuss these questions with a partner. Are you afraid of snakes? Why or why not? Are you afraid of any other animals? Explain your reasons.

## Grammar: *May, might,* and *could* for possibility

| Use *may, might,* and *could* + base verb to say that something is possible, now or in the future. | We **may find** dangerous animals in the jungle.<br>Monkeys **might learn** to be afraid of things.<br>People **could develop** a fear of snakes. |
| --- | --- |
| Use *may, might,* and *could* to express that we are not completely sure about something. | Scientists say that other fears **are** learned. (The scientists are sure about this.)<br>Scientists say that other fears **might be** learned. (The scientists are not sure about this, but it's possible.) |

**A** Why are these people afraid? Complete each sentence in your notebook with *may*, *might*, or *could* and a phrase from the box.

> get on the wrong train   see a snake   have an accident
> need a filling in my tooth   fall off   make a mistake

1. I don't like to walk across high bridges because <u>I could fall off.</u>

2. Jose Luis is afraid of speaking English because _____
   _____

3. My grandmother gets nervous when she's driving because _____
   _____

4. I don't like camping because _____

5. Nancy never takes the subway because _____

6. I worry about going to the dentist because _____

**B** 🔁 What are you afraid of? Tell your partner, and explain the reasons with *may*, *might*, or *could*.

## Conversation

**A** 🔊 **10** Listen to the conversation with your book closed. What is Andy afraid of?

**Susan:** You look really nervous, Andy. What's up?
**Andy:** Oh, I always feel like this before I take a trip. I hate flying!
**Susan:** Really? But you travel a lot!
**Andy:** I never feel comfortable. The plane might fly into bad weather, or the pilot could make a mistake.
**Susan:** I used to be afraid of flying too, but I got over it.
**Andy:** Really? How?
**Susan:** Listening to music on the plane makes me feel calm.

**B** 🔁 Practice the conversation in exercise **A** with a partner. Then make new conversations using the list below. Use your own ideas for ways to get over these fears.

> swimming in deep water   being in high places
> speaking in front of the class   visiting the doctor/dentist

**C** 🔁 **GOAL CHECK** ✓ **Talk about your fears**

Tell your partner about something you're afraid of. Why are you afraid of it?

**Wooden stairs descending into cave**

## Reading

**A** 🔄 Discuss these questions with a partner.

1. What happened to the person in the photo? Why does he feel like this?

2. What other emotions are there?

**B** Circle **T** for *true*, **F** for *false*, and **NI** for *no information* (if not in the reading).

1. Paul Ekman studied people's faces in different cultures. **T F NI**

2. Ekman did research in several countries and got different results. **T F NI**

3. Americans get angry more often than the Fore people from New Guinea. **T F NI**

4. Ekman thinks that emotions are the same everywhere because they are a part of our brain. **T F NI**

5. Two people might feel different emotions about the same thing. **T F NI**

6. Fear is the most difficult emotion to change. **T F NI**

**C** Look back at the reading and think about the meaning of the words in bold. Circle the answers.

1. If you do something *in reverse*, you do it again ( the same way | the opposite way ).

2. If something is *universal*, it's ( the same | different ) in every country.

3. When you *deal* with a problem, you ( take action | don't think about it ).

4. An emotional *trigger* makes an emotion ( happen | stop ).

San Francisco, California, USA

# IN YOUR FACE

Why is this man so angry? We don't know the reason, but we can see the emotion in his face. Whatever culture you come from, you can understand the feeling that he is expressing.

Forty years ago, psychologist Paul Ekman of the University of California, San Francisco, became interested in how people's faces show their feelings. He took photographs of Americans expressing various emotions. Then he showed them to the Fore people, who live in the jungle in New Guinea. Most of the Fore had never seen foreign faces, but they easily understood Americans' expressions of anger, happiness, sadness, disgust, fear, and surprise.

Then Ekman did the same experiment **in reverse**. He showed pictures of Fore faces to Americans, and the results were similar. Americans had no problem reading the emotions on the Fore people's faces. Ekman's research gave powerful support to the theory that facial expressions for basic emotions are the same everywhere. He did more research in Japan, Brazil, and Argentina, and got the same results. According to Ekman, these six emotions are **universal** because they are built into our brains. They developed to help us **deal** with things quickly that might hurt us. Some emotional triggers are universal as well. When something suddenly comes into sight, people feel fear, because it might be dangerous. But most emotional **triggers** are learned. For example, two people might smell newly cut grass. One person spent wonderful summers in the country as a child, so the smell makes him happy. The other person remembers working very hard on a farm and being hungry, so he feels sad.

Once we make an emotional association in our brain, it is difficult, and sometimes impossible, to change it. "Emotion is the least changeable part of the brain," says Ekman. But we can learn to manage our emotions better.

There are many differences between cultures in language and customs. But a smile is exactly the same everywhere.

## GOAL 4: Describe an Emotional Experience

Three children are surprised by a lizard.

| happiness | fear |
| --- | --- |
| surprise | sadness |
| anger | disgust |

## Communication

**A** Think about a time when you felt one of the emotions in the box. Tell your partner about your experience. Your partner will ask you for more details.

1. What happened?

2. How did you feel?

3. What did you do?

4. What did you learn from the experience?

## Writing

**A** In your notebook, write a paragraph about the experience you described in the Communication exercise. Include a topic sentence and interesting details. Use *and, but, or,* and *so* to connect your ideas.

**B** Share your writing with a different partner or with the entire class. Your partner or classmates will tell you what they liked about your paragraph.

**C** **GOAL CHECK** ✔ **Describe an emotional experience**

Write each emotion from the box in exercise **A** on a small piece of paper. Mix up the pieces and place them facedown. Take turns choosing a piece of paper and talking about a time when you had that emotion. The first pair of students to finish talking about all six emotions wins.

### Word Focus

You can use a variety of verbs to describe experiences.

**observe**
**notice**
**sense**
**perceive**
**imagine**
**become aware of**

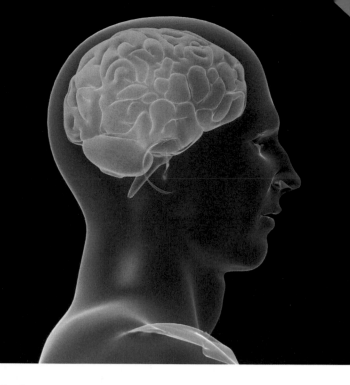

**How does memory work?**

When we get new information, it goes into a part of the brain called the **hippocampus.** There the information is **coded** and put into memory. But why are some people better at remembering? Some scientists think a good memory comes from **heredity.** We get it from our parents through their **genes.** Other people say a good memory comes from practice.

## Before You Watch

**A** Read the information in the box and study the words in **bold.**

## While You Watch

**A ▶** Watch the video. Complete the sentences.

1  Gianni Golfera is blindfolded, but he can still do something that's _____
   _____ .

2. He has memorized more than _____ books.

3. Researchers are studying how memory and _____ change the brain.

4. For Gianni, improving his memory has become a _____ .

5. Gianni's life is not all about _____ , though.

6. Gianni's practice is making his memory _____ .

## After You Watch/Communication

**A** Discuss these questions with a partner. Why do you think Gianni Golfera has such a good memory? Would you like to take Gianni's memory class? Explain your reasons.

Follow the steps to play a famous memory game.

1. Choose twelve small objects. Put them on top of a desk and cover them.

2. Go to another desk. In one minute, memorize the objects you see.

3. List all the objects you can remember in two minutes. Check your lists. Who remembered the most objects?

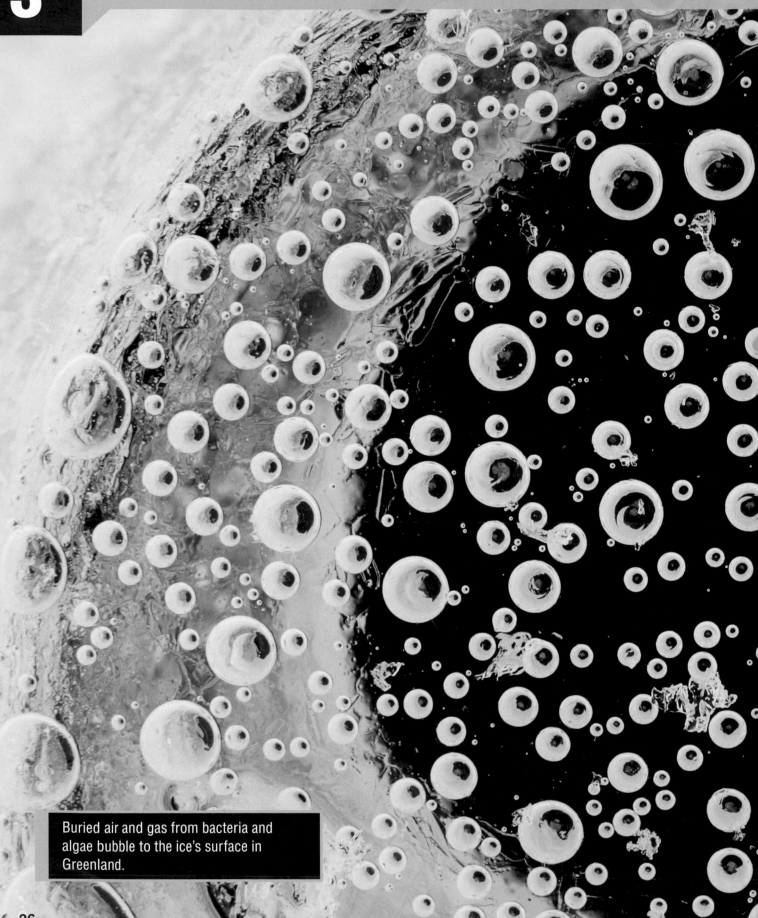

Buried air and gas from bacteria and algae bubble to the ice's surface in Greenland.

## UNIT 3 GOALS

**1.** Suggest solutions to environmental problems

**2.** Discuss causes and effects

**3.** Talk about invasive species

**4.** Discuss effects on the future

27

▲ Access roads and terraced fields in Sarawak, Borneo, Malaysia

## Vocabulary

**A** Read the article below from an environmental magazine.

### A New Mother Earth?

The Earth is changing fast—with a little help from people, of course. Our use of coal and oil for energy has led to global warming. This warming has led to an increase in temperatures and sea levels, and much less polar ice. But warming is not the only effect on the planet. Climate change means more extreme weather of all kinds: heat, cold, rain, and drought.

The effects of human activity can also be seen in the planet's plant and animal life. Demand for tree products and farmland leads to deforestation, and global travel provides easy transportation for invasive species—plants and animals that are brought in from other places.

Fortunately, even though we humans are the cause, we can also be part of the solution. We can use much less coal and oil if we practice conservation, for example, and better land management would save forests from being destroyed. Invasive plants and animals can even be controlled, but only with a good understanding of the environment.

**B** Write each word in blue next to its definition in your notebook.

1. a thick liquid used as a fuel
2. very great in degree or intensity
3. the cutting down of forests
4. a period with much less rain
5. protecting the environment
6. amount becoming greater
7. rise in Earth's temperature
8. the average water levels
9. caused, resulted in
10. a change in weather patterns

## Grammar: The passive

| | |
|---|---|
| Form the passive with *be* + the past participle of the main verb. | Often, trees **are removed** to make room for farming. |
| We can use the passive with any verb tense. | Thousands of acres of forest **have been destroyed** in recent years. |
| Use the passive:<br>1. when the agent (the doer) is not known or not important.<br>2. to emphasize the object of the verb. | Oil can **be refined** into gasoline and diesel fuel for cars, trucks, and ships.<br>Six countries in the region **were affected** by drought last year. |
| Use a *by* phrase to say who or what does something (the agent). | New trees <u>are being planted</u> **by local children.** |

**A** Rewrite sentences in your notebook in the passive. Use a *by* phrase when needed.

1. People use coal and oil for heating and transportation.

2. <u>Conservation groups</u> raise money for environmental projects.

3. Extreme weather has caused many problems in recent years.

4. <u>Immigrants</u> brought invasive species to Australia during the 1800s.

5. <u>Palm oil plantations</u> are causing deforestation in Southeast Asia.

6. In many parts of the world, people are conserving energy.

7. <u>One company</u> developed an excellent land management plan.

8. <u>Recycling</u> has kept tons of paper and plastic out of landfills.

**B** Complete the sentences with an appropriate agent.

1. Those nests in that tree were made by _____ .

2. This textbook was published by _____ .

3. Oil is being used as fuel by _____ .

4. My favorite kind of shampoo is made by _____ .

5. Rising sea levels are caused by _____ .

## Conversation

**A** 🔊 **11** Close your book and listen to the conversation. What does Pedro think should be done about climate change?

**Sonia:** Hey, what's up? You look worried.
**Pedro:** I am worried.
**Sonia:** About what?
**Pedro:** I hear a lot about climate change, but I feel like nothing is being done about it.
**Sonia:** I know what you mean, but what do you think should be done?
**Pedro:** Well, look at this neighborhood. More trees could be planted.
**Sonia:** Would that help?
**Pedro:** Definitely! Trees keep cities cooler, so they don't become heat islands.
**Sonia:** Heat islands! I learn something new every day.

**B** 🔁 Practice the conversation with a partner. Make new conversations with your own ideas for solving the climate change problem.

**C** 🔗 Discuss how climate change is affecting your country. Make a list of things that are being done about it (or that could be done) where you live.

**D** 🔗 **GOAL CHECK** ✔ **Suggest solutions to environmental problems**

Share your group's list from exercise **C** with the class.

### Real Language

When you have a *heat wave*, you have days or weeks of extreme heat.

> Laws have been passed to reduce pollution from cars.

> Right. We can only drive on certain days of the week.

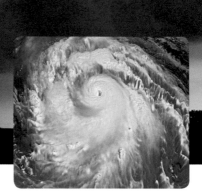

1. _____

2. _____

3. _____

4. _____

## Listening

**A** 🔁 Rank these types of extreme weather from most serious (1) to least serious (5) in your opinion. Then compare your rankings with a partner.

_____ floods

_____ very cold weather

_____ hurricanes/typhoons

_____ drought

_____ very hot weather

**B** 🔊 **12** Listen to four people talk about climate change. Write the name of a place below each picture on the left.

**C** 🔊 **12** Listen again. Answer each question in your notebook.

1. According to Mari, what is happening to the cattle?

2. How many deaths occurred in Europe during one heat wave?

3. Why do some scientists say that global warming isn't causing the heat waves?

4. According to Joseph, how many hurricanes and tropical storms occurred one year?

5. How does warm ocean water cause strong storms?

6. How are recent floods in Jasmine's country different than in the past?

## Pronunciation: Linking words together

When a word ends in a consonant sound and the next word begins with a vowel sound, the words are linked together.

*What's the capital of Japan?* (Can you hear the word *of*?)

When a word ends in a consonant sound and the next word begins with the same consonant sound, the words are linked and the sound is only pronounced once.

*We didn't feel like going home, so we went to the museum.* (Can you hear *fee-like* and *wen-to*?)

**A** 🔊 **13** Underline the sounds that link together. Then listen and check your answers.

1. Climate change has been in the news lately.

2. We've received dozens of letters.

3. Will this rain never end?

4. The heat takes a toll on the human body.

5. The governor is worried about food shortages.

6. Is that a good way to save energy?

**B** 🖉 Write sentences using these word pairs in your notebook. Then practice saying the sentences with a partner.

1. weather report
2. gone over
3. above average
4. coldest temperatures
5. drought ended
6. more rainfall

## Communication

**A** 🖉 How do these things happen? Match the causes with their effects.

| Causes | Effects |
|---|---|
| 1. burning coal and oil | a. rising sea levels |
| 2. deforestation | b. invasive species |
| 3. movement of people and goods | c. pollution in the atmosphere |
| 4. climate change | d. fewer trees |
| 5. increasing temperatures | e. more extreme weather |

**B** 👥 Compare answers with another pair. Does everyone agree?

**C** 👥 **GOAL CHECK** ✔ **Discuss causes and effects**

Make a list of things you do every day that affect the environment. Then explain your list to the class.

Air pollution is caused by burning coal and oil.

Yes, and air pollution causes an increase in temperatures.

## Language Expansion: Large numbers

| Saying Large Numbers | |
|---|---|
| To say large numbers in English, start at the left, and say the numbers in groups: | |
| **hundreds (100s)** | 524 → five hundred (and) twenty-four |
| **thousands (1,000s)** | 1,250 → one thousand, two hundred (and) fifty |
| **ten thousands (10,000s)** | 17,400 → seventeen thousand (and) four hundred |
| **hundred thousands (100,000s)** | 432,060 → four hundred thirty-two thousand (and) sixty |
| **millions (1,000,000s)** | 2,400,900 → two million, four hundred thousand (and) nine hundred |

▲ Royal penguins returning to their colony in Macquarie Island, Australia

**A** 🔁 Discuss these questions with a partner.

1. What are invasive species? Can you think of an example?

2. Why are invasive species a problem?

**B** Read about Macquarie Island. Guess which number is correct.

> What do you think? 8,000, 80,000, or 800,000?

> I think it's 8,000.

Like many places, Macquarie Island has invasive species—species of nonnative plants and animals with no local natural controls on their populations. First came the cats, which were used on ships to control rats. Then came the rabbits, which were brought by seal hunters as a source of food. The hunters came because Macquarie Island is visited by around **(8,000/80,000/800,000)** elephant seals each year. No hunting is allowed now, however, because the island is a wildlife sanctuary.

Macquarie Island has also been an accidental sanctuary for its invasive species. The rabbits found plenty to eat, and they ate an enormous amount of the island's plant life. In 1968, scientists wanted to decrease the rabbit population, so the European rabbit flea (which carries a virus called myxomatosis) was introduced. By the 1980s, the rabbit population had declined from **(1,300/13,000/130,000)** to only **(2,000/20,000/200,000)**, and the vegetation on the island had begun to recover. But with fewer rabbits to eat, the cats began to prey on the island's sea birds, so scientists decided to kill the island's cats.

Problem solved? Unfortunately, the virus had only reduced the rabbit population, and with the cats gone, the rabbits' numbers increased again. Now that so much of the island's vegetation is gone, there have been landslides after heavy rains. One expert estimates that it will cost **($162,000/$1,620,000/$16,200,000)** to finally solve the invasive species problem on Macquarie Island.

**C** 🔁 Take turns asking about the numbers in the article.

## Grammar: The past perfect

| Use the past perfect tense to talk about something that happened before another event in the past.<br>subject + **had** + **(not)** + **past participle** | The game warden arrived on Wednesday and saw that many fish **had died.**<br>They **had not had** problems in that lake previously. |
| --- | --- |
| The simple past tense is often used with words such as *before* or *after* that make the time relationship clear. Both forms are grammatically correct. | Cats **had come** to the island on ships **before** the rabbits arrived.<br>Cats **came** to the island on ships **before** the rabbits arrived. |

**A** Read each sentence and underline what happens first.

1. The Nile Perch had been a river fish before it was brought to Lake Victoria.

2. The lake had not had such a large predator before the perch arrived.

3. By the late 1980s, the perch population had grown enormously.

4. James called his mother after he finished playing soccer.

5. Before the sun went down, Rita found a good place to watch the fireworks.

**B** Read the article about Macquarie Island again and underline the verbs in the past perfect tense. Why is the past perfect used in those sentences?

## Conversation

**A** 🔊 **14** Close your book and listen to the conversation. What does Henry want to do?

**Abdullah:** Look at this, Henry.
**Henry:** Eeeew . . . What is it?
**Abdullah:** I'm not sure. It's some kind of insect, but I've never seen one like it.
**Henry:** Maybe it came here on a ship—in a box of food.
**Abdullah:** Right! The ship had probably been to another country to pick up . . . carrots!
**Henry:** Sure. And after that, the ship came here.
**Abdullah:** And now our country will be invaded by the terrible Carrot Beetle!
**Henry:** Not if we do something about it first.
**Abdullah:** Hold on, Henry. We can't kill it if we don't even know what it is.
**Henry:** You're right. Maybe we should show it to the biology teacher.

▲ Leaf beetle

**B** 🗘 Practice the conversation. Have new conversations about invasive species in your city with a partner.

**C** 🗘 | **GOAL CHECK** ✓ **Talk about invasive species**

With a partner, discuss the events on Macquarie Island in your own words. What had the island been like before people arrived? What problem did each new species cause?

**GOAL 4:** Discuss Effects on the Future

## Reading

**A** 🔁 Check (✓) the actions in the list that can affect our future. Share your ideas with a partner.

_____ **1.** If everyone drives their own car, we might run out of fuel.

_____ **2.** If we use energy-efficient light bulbs, we will use less electricity.

_____ **3.** If the world's population keeps growing, we might not have enough food and water.

_____ **4.** If we protect wilderness areas, we can save endangered species.

_____ **5.** If we use biofuels, we might reduce $CO_2$ emissions.

**B** 🔁 Read the text. Match the actions with the results. Compare your answers.

_____ **1.** Make small changes in how we use energy

_____ **2.** Use renewable biofuels

_____ **3.** Paint building roofs white

_____ **4.** Know the ecological cost of our choices

**a.** Make decisions that are good for the future

**b.** Save money on lighting and air conditioning

**c.** Have a big impact on the planet

**d.** Keep tons of $CO_2$ out of the air

**C** Complete the sentences.

**1.** John Doerr's main job is in finance, but he is also interested in _____ .

**2.** A compact fluorescent light bulb can last as long as _____ years.

**3.** In _____, 40% of vehicles use biofuels instead of gasoline.

**4.** According to Doerr, companies can also help the environment by changing the way they use _____ .

**John Doerr** Venture Capitalist

# SALVATION (AND PROFIT) IN GREENTECH

John Doerr might not be the first person you think of when you make a list of environmental activists. He is better known as a "money man" in Silicon Valley, where he invested in big companies like Amazon and Google.

But Doerr is also passionate about saving the planet. He and his business colleagues have spent a lot of time studying "green technology." He has learned that when businesses and individuals make even small changes in the way they use energy, it can have a big impact on the planet. Doerr believes that businesses, individuals, and governments all need to be involved to solve environmental problems, and that it will require exciting and radical innovations.

One of the biggest changes everyone can make, Doerr says, is to switch the light bulbs in their houses to energy-efficient bulbs, which are also called "compact fluorescent bulbs." These light bulbs use three to five times less energy than regular light bulbs, which reduces $CO_2$ emissions, and they last much longer—some can last up to eight years! They are more expensive than regular bulbs, but the energy they save over time makes up for the difference in price.

Doerr recommends using more renewable biofuels in our cars and trucks. Very few vehicles in the world run on these special fuels right now. However, some countries are making it easier for drivers to use them. In Brazil, for example, about 40% of vehicles use biofuels, which keeps millions of tons of $CO_2$ out of the air. And researchers are working to develop better biofuels all the time, which will save more energy, keep the air cleaner, and make the planet healthier.

Companies can make changes that impact the environment, too. A large chain of retail stores painted the roofs of about 25% of their buildings white and

"I really, really hope that we multiply all of our energy, all of our talent, and all of our influence to solve this problem."

Global warming?

John Doerr's idea worth spreading is that being green is the most important thing anyone can do. And we need to do it more—right now. Watch Doerr's full TED Talk on TED.com.

installed skylights. As a result, they saved money on lighting and air-conditioning, and reduced the $CO_2$ emissions associated with those energy uses.

In order to make decisions that will affect the future in positive ways, we need to know as consumers how much our choices cost, Doerr says. Those costs can be financial, like the price of a light bulb or a liter of fuel, or they can be environmental. Did you ever wonder how much $CO_2$ it takes to put water in a plastic bottle and to transport it from its source to your refrigerator? By asking the right questions, we can make the right decisions.

**impact**  *a powerful or major influence or effect*
**renewable**  *able to be replaced by nature*
**biofuel**  *a material produced from plants that is burned to produce heat or power*
**CO₂**  *a gas that is produced when people and animals breathe out or when certain fuels are burned, and that is used by plants for energy: carbon dioxide*
**skylight**  *a window in the roof of a house or on a ship's deck*

▲ $CO_2$ is generated when bottled water is moved from the source to the store.

## Communication

**A** 🔄 Think about actions and their environmental impact that can affect the future. Rank them from most positive to most negative. Share your ideas with a partner.

## Writing

**A** Complete the sentences with the simple past or past perfect of the verbs.

1. After we _____ (receive) a huge electric bill, we _____ (decided) to change all of our light bulbs to compact fluorescents.

2. John Doerr _____ (work) in finance for many years before he _____ (become) concerned with protecting the environment and preventing climate change.

3. By 2007, many vehicles in Brazil _____ (change) to using biofuels.

**B** Rewrite the newspaper article in the box by changing the underlined text to the passive voice in your notebook.

**C** Write a news article about actions we can take to affect the environment in a positive way. Remember to use the passive voice.

**D** ♻ **GOAL CHECK** ✔ **Discuss Effects on the Future**

Share your rankings of actions that affect the future. Brainstorm two more positive and negative actions. Who is responsible for these actions? Doerr mentions individuals, businesses, and governments. What could each group do about these actions?

---

(1) The government released a new report yesterday. It showed how (2) our actions have clear effects on the environment. (3) We save energy when we switch to compact fluorescent bulbs. Bigger changes were also reported, such as when (4) stores reduce $CO_2$ emissions because they make changes to their buildings. (5) Finally, the report says that even small actions create important impacts.

**A canal in Amsterdam**

## Before You Watch

**A** Read some quick facts about the Netherlands.

- Another name for the Netherlands is Holland.

- About half of the country's land is below sea level.

- The Dutch have built walls called *dikes* between the sea and the land. They have created new areas of dry land.

- Windmills move water to the sea, and as the water is removed, the land **sinks** even lower.

- As sea levels **rise** due to global warming, the Dutch must decide how to deal with the rising water. Should they continue to **struggle** against the sea?

## While You Watch

**A** ▶ Watch the video and choose the best phrase to complete each sentence.

1. Instead of fighting the sea, it might be necessary to _____.
   **a.** struggle against the sea          **b.** give land back to the sea

2. Flood control lakes could be used for _____.
   **a.** recreation and wildlife           **b.** farmland

3. Older Dutch people don't like the idea because they think _____.
   **a.** fighting the water is necessary    **b.** water makes a pretty landscape

## After You Watch/Communication

**A** 🔁 What are the advantages of letting some of the land in the Netherlands fill up with water? What are the disadvantages?

## Before You Watch

**A** Look at the picture and answer the questions with a partner.

1. What do you think it would be like to grow up in a place like this?

2. How would it be different from where you live?

3. What types of things could you learn from living in this type of environment?

**B** How much do you know about climate change? Mark each item *True* or *False*. Compare your answers with a partner.

1. Climate change is caused by the sun's activity, not by human activity. _____

2. A change of only one or two degrees in global average temperatures can have a major effect on our lives. _____

3. A small rise in sea level will have a major impact on animals like polar bears. _____

4. A small rise in sea level will have a significant impact on people. _____

5. Melting polar ice will not affect me. _____

6. It is too late to do anything about climate change. _____

**C** Here are some words you will hear in the Ted Talk. Complete the paragraph with the correct words. Not all words will be used.

Paul Nicklen's idea worth spreading is that the loss of polar ice could devastate entire ecosystems, including the remarkable animals that inhabit them. Watch Nicklen's full TED Talk on TED.com.

**dejected** *adj.* sad
**feed** *v.* give food to; eat
**Inuit** *n.* native people of Canada
**grab** *v.* take, catch
**starve** *v.* die from lack of food
**threat** *n.* danger

Global warming is a (1) _____ to many animals. For example, emperor penguins live on Antarctic ice. If the ice melts, this will impact the penguins and also the animals that eat them. For example, leopard seals eat these penguins. If the penguins disappear, the seals will not be able to (2) _____ their babies and may (3) _____. Global warming is a serious and complicated problem. It makes many people feel (4)_ _____.

**D** You are going to watch a TED Talk about Paul Nicklen's adventures in Antarctica. What do you think you will see in the video? Discuss with a partner.

**E** Watch the TED Talk. Put the quotes on Page 39 in order that you hear them. Write the number in the boxes provided.

**F** Watch the talk again. Put these events in order.

__1__ **a.** Paul goes to Antarctica.

____ **b.** A leopard seal brings Paul a live penguin.

____ **c.** Paul's family moves to Northern Canada.

____ **d.** The seal makes a threat display to another seal to protect Paul.

____ **e.** Paul becomes interested in polar areas.

"So what I'm trying to do with my work is [make] people understand... that if we lose ice, we stand to lose an entire ecosystem." – Paul Nicklen

"The leopard seal did this threat display for a few minutes and then the most amazing thing happened. She totally relaxed."

"The penguin doesn't know it's cute and the leopard seal doesn't know it's big and monstrous; this is just the food chain unfolding."

"I was laughing so hard, and [I was] so emotional, that my mask was flooding because I was crying underwater just because it was so amazing."

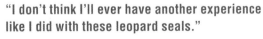

"I don't think I'll ever have another experience like I did with these leopard seals."

**Challenge!** Can you paraphrase the quotes from Paul Nicklen? Take turns with a partner.

## After You Watch

**A** Mark each statement *True* or *False*. Correct the false statements in your notebook.

1. As a boy, Paul learned about nature from TV and computers. _____

2. Paul says people don't like leopard seals. He travels to Antarctica to find out more about them. _____

3. The second time the seal made a threat display, she wanted to bite Paul. _____

4. The seal only tried to feed Paul once, then gave up. _____

5. Paul had a bad experience in Antarctica with the penguins. _____

6. In Antarctica, Paul learned that leopard seals are not vicious (dangerous); they are misunderstood. _____

**B** Fill in the blank with the correct verb form.

1. Paul Nicklen _____ (has worked / had worked) with polar animals for years.

2. He _____ (was taught / has taught) about these animals by the Inuit people he lived with in Canada.

3. Paul is worried that global warming _____ (may have / has) a negative effect on species like the leopard seal and the polar bear.

4. _____ (To take / Taking) pictures of polar animals is his way of putting faces to the crisis of climate change.

5. His pictures _____ (are published / could publish) in *National Geographic* Magazine.

6. Paul wants people _____ (knowing / to know) the wonderful animals that inhabit the polar regions.

**C** 🔁 With a partner, role-play an interview with Paul Nicklen. You will switch roles to each answer as Paul.

STUDENT 1 ASKS:

1. Paul, can you tell me about when you moved to Northern Canada?

2. Why did you become interested in leopard seals?

3. What were you thinking on the boat before you got in the water with a seal for the first time?

STUDENT 2 ASKS:

1. What was the most amazing moment you had with the leopard seals?

2. Why is it important to protect the polar regions?

3. Why are you worried about ice disappearing ?

**Paul Nicklen encounters a leopard seal.**

**D** 👥 Survey your classmates. Write a question for each item. Ask a different person each question. Ask a follow-up question for more details. Answer your classmates' questions.

- Andrea, have you ever lived in a different place?
- Yes, when I was 15.
- Where did you move?

|  | Question | Name | Details |
|---|---|---|---|
| **1.** live in a different place |  |  |  |
| **2.** experience an extreme climate |  |  |  |
| **3.** describe an incredible photo |  |  |  |
| **4.** worry about climate change |  |  |  |
| **5.** see an endangered animal |  |  |  |

**Challenge!** 👥 Paul Nicklen talks about many more animals in his TED Talk. In groups of three, research his work. Pick another one of his projects and prepare a short presentation.

• Watch the full TED Talk, or visit his Web site to find more stories.

• Write a short summary of the area/animal Paul studied.

• Assign each member of the group a portion of the presentation.

**Presentation Strategy**

Using Visuals

Paul Nicklen uses many photos to make his talk more interesting.

Tourists and buskers in Prague,
Czech Republic

**UNIT 4 GOALS**

1. Describe your financial habits

2. Discuss things that people value

3. Talk about banking

4. Talk about different types of wealth

43

## Vocabulary

**A** Read the statements below. Do you agree?

### MONEY

1. People should only borrow money if they want to buy something big, like a car.
2. It's always a bad idea to lend money to your friends.
3. I try to make a budget for how I will spend my money.
4. I prefer to pay in cash when I buy things.
5. Young people can have debt because they can pay it back in the future.
6. For me, a good income is more important than an interesting job.
7. I'm careful with money, and I enjoy finding a bargain when I go shopping.
8. My living expenses are very high.

**B** Write the words in blue next to their correct meanings in your notebook.

1. money in coins and bills
2. to receive a loan that you will return
3. money that you spend
4. a plan for spending your money
5. to give money to a person for a period of time
6. money that you receive for working
7. something good for a low price
8. money owed to a bank or a company

**C** Compare your answers in exercise **A** with a partner's answers.

## Grammar: Gerund vs. infinitive

| | |
|---|---|
| **Verb + infinitive**<br>We use infinitives after certain verbs, including:<br>hope   try   want   learn   need   promise   decide   agree | *I **try to make** a budget for how I will spend my money.* |
| **Verb + gerund**<br>We use gerunds after certain verbs, including:<br>avoid   enjoy   stop   finish   give up   consider | *I **enjoy finding** a bargain when I go shopping.* |
| **Verb + infinitive or gerund**<br>We can use infinitives or gerunds after certain verbs, including:<br>like   prefer   hate   begin   continue   love | *I **prefer to pay** in cash. Or I **prefer paying** in cash.* |

**A** Complete the sentences with the infinitive or gerund of the verb in parentheses.

1. I decided _____ (save) money for a new computer.

2. Mark agreed _____ (work) on Saturdays so he can have Mondays off.

3. I stopped _____ (eat) in restaurants, and I learned _____ (cook) simple meals.

4. Loren hopes _____ (study) in Australia next year.

5. If you are in debt, you should avoid _____ (borrow) more money.

6. I'm trying _____ (get) a different job so I can have a higher income.

> I hope to buy a car next year.

> Really? What kind of car?

**B** 🗣 Tell your partner about your money habits using the verbs in the box with gerunds or infinitives. Ask questions about things your partner says.

> I love . . .    I hope . . .
> I decided . . .    I stopped . . .
> I usually avoid . . .

## Conversation

**A** 🔊 **15** Listen to the conversation with your book closed. When does the man go out with his friends?

**Beth:** I love eating in restaurants, but it's so expensive now!

**Rick:** Yeah, I know. That's why I stopped going out for dinner. I meet my friends on Saturday at noon because lunch is a bargain at lots of places.

**Beth:** That's a good idea.

**Rick:** We like to eat in small, neighborhood restaurants. They're not so expensive.

**Beth:** And they usually have better food.

**Rick:** I think so, too. And one more thing—I avoid having dessert. That's another good way to save money.

**Beth:** You don't have dessert? That's a little too extreme for me!

**B** 🗣 Practice the conversation with a partner.

**C** 🗣 With your partner, list three ideas for how to save money on each of the things below. Make new conversations.

> food   clothes   vacations

**D** 👥 Share your money-saving ideas with the class.

**E** 🗣 **GOAL CHECK** ✔ **Describe your financial habits**

Are your money habits similar to your friends' habits or different? Tell a partner.

**Two gold coins, one showing the head of Nero, a Roman emperor**

## Listening

**A** 🔊 16 Listen to a radio program about the history of money. Circle the main idea of the program.

1. People have used many different things as money.

2. People's ideas about money have been the same for thousands of years.

3. Money causes different problems in people's lives.

**B** 🔊 16 Listen again and number the places on the map in the order that you hear about them.

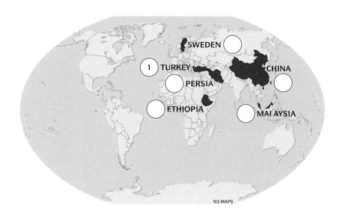

**C** 🔊 16 Listen again. Circle **T** for *true* and **F** for *false*.

1. Coins were made in Turkey about 3,000 years ago.                     T    F

2. Paper money is older than coins.                                      T    F

3. The people in Persia liked to use paper money because it was new.     T    F

4. Coins and bills are the only kinds of money.                          T    F

5. The Native Americans in North America had a form of money.            T    F

**D** 🔗 Discuss these questions with a partner.

1. Why do people want money? Talk about as many reasons as you can.

2. Does having more money always make people happier? Explain your answer.

## Pronunciation: Reduction of *to*

**A** 🔊 **17** The word *to* is usually pronounced very quickly, with a /ə/ sound. Circle the word *to* in these sentences, and then listen to the pronunciation.

1. The king told all the people to use paper money.

2. People began to use coins a long time ago.

3. I try to learn five English words every day.

4. I like to find a bargain when I go to the store.

5. He sent an e-mail to his parents to ask them for money.

6. We go to the library after class.

**B** 🔁 Read the sentences in exercise **A** to a partner. Pay attention to the pronunciation of *to*.

## Communication

**A** Read the saying. What do you think it means?

*The best things in life are free.*

**B** 🔁 Make a list of things you enjoy that don't cost any money. Then share your list with a partner.

**C** 👥 Your class is going to write a guidebook for people who want to have fun without spending money. Follow these steps:

1. With your group, list as many ideas as you can for fun activities that don't cost money in your notebook.

| Things to do at home | Things to do with your friends | Things to do in your city |
|---|---|---|
| | | |

2. Write your lists on the board.

3. With the class, choose the best ideas in each category.

**D** 👥 Which of the activities have you done? Which activities do you want to try?

**E** 🔁 **GOAL CHECK** ✔ **Discuss things that people value**

Work with a partner. Talk about things that people value in your country. Are these things different now than in the past? Why or why not?

## Language Expansion: Banking

**A** Label the pictures with words from the box.

| savings account | teller | PIN number | deposit | receipt | ATM | checking account | withdraw |

1. _____  2. _____  3. _____  4. _____

5. _____  6. _____  7. _____  8. _____

**B** Which of the things in exercise **A** do you have experience with?

## Grammar: Review of the passive voice

| | |
|---|---|
| Form the passive with:<br>Subject + *be* + past participle (+ *by* agent). | The money **is** usually **deposited** by the store manager. |
| Affirmative statement<br>Negative statement<br>*Yes/No* questions<br>*Wh-* questions | The receipt **will be printed** automatically.<br>Bank tellers **are not paid** very much.<br>**Are** credit cards **accepted** here?<br>Where **was** that coin **made**? |
| The focus of the passive is usually on the result of the action, not on who does the action (the agent). | Coffee **is grown** in Brazil (by farmers).<br>We **were not told** about the quiz (by the teacher). |
| Use the passive with any verb tense. Change the form of *be* to show the tense. | Lunch **is being served** on the terrace.<br>Gold coins **have been used** for a long time. |
| The agent, or *by* phrase, is included only if that information is important or surprising. | *Hamlet* **was written** by William Shakespeare. (important)<br>That movie **was made** by two teenagers. (surprising) |

**A** Read the article about how an ATM works, and fill in the verbs in the passive voice.

A man in Paris needs money from his bank in Washington. He goes to an ATM. In seconds, he receives 100 Euros from his savings account. How does this work?

The card (1) _____ (insert) into the machine, and the PIN (2) _____ (enter). The information (3) _____ (send) to the bank's computer. The computer sees that it's a foreign ATM card, so an electronic message (4) _____ (transmit) to the banking center in Belgium, and then to the center in Detroit, and finally to the bank in Washington. The account (5) _____ (check). If there is enough money in it, a message (6) _____ (return) to the ATM in Paris and the cash (7) _____ (deliver).

ATMs (8) _____ (invent) in the 1970s. At first, they (9) _____ (not use) very much. Now they (10) _____ (find) all around the world.

**B** 🗘 Work with a partner. Which of these sentences should include an agent? Why? Cross out the agent where it's not needed.

1. My computer was made ~~by factory workers~~ in Malaysia.
2. Our homework is collected every day by our teacher at the end of class.
3. I love to wear this dress because it was made by my grandmother.
4. While shopping in Central Market, Alex's wallet was stolen by a thief.
5. The ATM was introduced by Barclay's Bank.
6. The first paper money was used by the Chinese about 1,000 years ago.

## Conversation

**A** 🔊 18 Listen to the conversation with your book closed. How much money does the woman want?

**Teller:** Next? May I help you?
**Annie:** Yes. I need to withdraw $100.
**Teller:** Please fill out this form and write your account number here.
**Annie:** OK.
**Teller:** Do you want to withdraw the money from your savings account or your checking account?
**Annie:** From my checking account, please.
**Teller:** Here you are, $100. And here's your receipt. Have a good day.
**Annie:** Thank you. You, too.

**B** 🗘 You want to do the things in the box. Make new conversations.

**C** 🗘 **GOAL CHECK** ✔ **Talk about banking**

Do you think it's important to have a checking or savings account at a bank? Why or why not?

### Engage!

How often do you use an ATM? Why?

### Real Language

*Here you are.* People use this expression when they hand something to someone.

deposit $200 in your checking account

withdraw $150 from your savings account

## Reading

**A** 🔁 What things do you value most? Check (✓) the items in the list. Share your ideas.

_____ 1. lots of money

_____ 2. being healthy

_____ 3. a nice house

_____ 4. having a family

_____ 5. your passion (music, sports, nature, etc.)

_____ 6. helping others

**B** 🔁 Read the text. Circle the correct option. Compare your answers with a partner.

1. Robert Gupta is a talented ( doctor | musician ).

2. Nathaniel Ayers studied music ( at a school | on his own ).

3. Gupta is interested in ( money | science ) as well as music.

4. Ayers spent many years living ( on the streets | in a hotel ).

5. A ( journalist | actor ) named Steve Lopez wrote about Ayers.

**C** Write _True_ or _False_ next to the statements below.

_____ 1. Robert Gupta began to play with the Los Angeles Philharmonic when he was 19.

_____ 2. Gupta met Nathaniel Ayers on the streets of Los Angeles.

_____ 3. A movie was made about Gupta's life.

_____ 4. Ayers works as a professional musician now.

_____ 5. Gupta will play music with Ayers any time he can.

## TED Ideas worth spreading

**Robert Gupta** Violinist, Mental Health Activist

# MUSIC IS MEDICINE, MUSIC IS SANITY

Even though some people believe that money makes the world go around, many people would choose health over wealth, opinion polls tell us. For someone like violinist Robert Gupta, who was on his way to becoming a physician before joining the Los Angeles Philharmonic at age 19, music, health, and wealth are all part of the same package.

In addition to music, Gupta is deeply interested in neurobiology. Because of his dual interests, he has had the chance to work with Nathaniel Anthony Ayers, a talented musician whose career was sidelined by **schizophrenia.** Although Ayers studied music at the Juilliard School in New York City, his mental illness got in the way of professional success.

After dropping out of Juilliard and having unsuccessful medical treatment for his schizophrenia, Ayers moved to Los Angeles where he ended up **homeless.** In 2005, a journalist for the _Los Angeles Times_ named Steve Lopez heard Ayers playing music in the streets. Lopez wrote a book about Ayers and became his friend. Their friendship became the subject of a movie, and because of the book and the movie, Ayers has had a chance to perform his music in some of the most famous concert halls in the world.

It seemed like Ayers had found his happy ending. However, he refuses to take medication to treat his schizophrenia. He says it keeps him from "hearing the music." Because of this, Ayers is still **prone** to schizophrenic episodes and sometimes leaves his home to go back to the streets.

Gupta was introduced to Ayers after Lopez took his friend to a performance of Beethoven's First and Fourth **symphonies,** and Ayers asked Gupta for a violin lesson. When they first met, Ayers was agitated and on edge. Gupta was afraid that if he taught the

"The redemptive power of music brought him back into a family of musicians that understood him, that recognized his talents and respected him."

Robert Gupta's idea worth spreading is that music can be medicine. Watch Gupta's full TED Talk on TED.com.

lesson in his usual way, Ayers would react violently. Finally, he just began playing. A change came over Ayers. Gupta said, "And in a miracle, he lifted his own violin and he started playing." The two musicians played many violin pieces together that day. A **bond** was formed.

Music, Gupta realized, is a way to deal with our emotions, even our most unpleasant ones. "This was the very reason why we made music (. . .) through our creativity, we're able to shape those emotions into reality," he says.

Now, Gupta says, "I will always make music with Nathaniel, whether we're at Walt Disney Concert Hall or on Skid Row, because he reminds me why I became a musician."

**schizophrenia** *a very serious mental illness in which someone cannot think or behave normally and often experiences delusions*
**homeless** *having no place to live*
**prone** *likely to do, have, or suffer from something*
**symphony** *a long piece of music that is usually in four large, separate sections and that is performed by an orchestra*
**bond** *something (such as an idea, interest, experience, or feeling) that is shared and forms a connection between people*

Music is important to many people, whether they are listening to it or playing it.

When he was young, Robert Gupta hoped (1) _____ (become) a doctor. However, he also loved (2) _____ (play) the violin. He finally decided (3) _____ (follow) his heart, becoming a professional musician when he was 19. One day, Gupta met Nathaniel Ayers, who was also a talented musician. However, because of mental illness, Ayers had given up (4) _____ (study) music. Gupta and Ayers played violin together, and Gupta saw that Ayers enjoyed (5) _____ (play) music for the music alone, not for money or fame. Gupta realized that music was more valuable to Ayers than anything else.

## Communication

**A** 🔁 Think about the things that are valuable to you in life. How many of them can be bought with money? How many cannot?

## Writing

**A** Complete the sentences with the passive form of the verbs.

1. Nathaniel Ayers _____ (discover) playing music on the streets.

2. His story _____ (tell) by journalist Steve Lopez.

3. A movie _____ (make) about Nathaniel Ayers in 2009.

4. Gupta and Ayers _____ (introduce) after a concert in L.A.

5. After they played together, a bond _____ (form) between Ayers and Gupta.

**B** Complete the paragraph in the box with the gerund or the infinitive.

**C** Write a paragraph about the things that you value in life. Be sure to use gerunds and infinitives.

**D** 👥 **GOAL CHECK** ✔️ **Talk about different types of wealth**

Share your ideas about what is valuable to you. Do you value music in the way that Gupta and Ayers do? What other things are valuable to you, and why? Give reasons for your opinions.

Marketplace in Marrakech

## Before You Watch

**A** 🔗 You are going to watch a video about shopping in a marketplace in Morocco. What do you think people can buy there? List your ideas in your notebook.

## While You Watch

**A** ▶ Watch the video *Making a Deal*. Circle the things you see from your list.

**B** ▶ Watch the video again. Circle **T** for *true* or **F** for *false*. Correct the false sentences in your notebook.

1. In the souk, only the seller decides the price. **T   F**
2. Foreigners and Moroccans pay different prices in the market. **T   F**
3. If you aren't good at bargaining, you might pay 10 percent more. **T   F**
4. The vendors are trying to steal money from the shoppers. **T   F**
5. The hat shop is the most difficult place for tourists. **T   F**
6. Tourists can learn how to bargain by watching Moroccans. **T   F**

## After You Watch/Communication

**A** 🔗 Discuss the questions with a partner. Do you think bargaining for prices is a good system? Explain your reasons. Have you ever bargained for something? Talk about your experience.

**B** 🔗 Try selling something by bargaining! Choose something you have with you now, such as your watch or cell phone. Think of a description and decide on the price you would like to sell it for. Show the item to a partner and describe it. Bargain until you agree on a price. Tell the class about the things you "bought" and "sold."

A green sea turtle hatchling runs to the sea leaving tiny tracks in Bentota, Sri Lanka.

**UNIT 5 GOALS**

**1.** Talk about emergency situations

**2.** Evaluate survival methods

**3.** Describe how animals survive

**4.** Write a brochure

▲ natural disaster

## Vocabulary

**A** Read part of a survival brochure. Notice the words in blue.

**Survival Advice**

According to experts, there are several things you can do to increase your chances of survival in an emergency such as a fire, or a natural disaster such as an earthquake.

- Preparation can be the key to survival. Be sure you have food, water, and other supplies in your home. Having a backpack prepared for family members is a good idea in case you have to evacuate quickly.
- Before going camping, hiking, or mountain climbing, make sure you have the proper equipment. Tents, sleeping bags, and a first-aid kit can save your life in case of bad weather, injury, or illness.
- Staying calm can help you cope with any emergency situation. Swimmers, for example, sometimes get caught in strong ocean currents. If they panic, they may become exhausted and unable to swim. If they relax and swim slowly, they will have the energy to swim to shore once they are out of the current.

### Word Focus

To **cope with** a situation means to deal with it successfully.

**B** Discuss these questions with a partner.

1. What kinds of natural disasters can happen where you live?

2. What equipment and supplies do people need to survive natural disasters?

3. What kind of emergency situation have you experienced in your life?

4. What happens when people panic in emergency situations?

5. What kind of preparation helps people to be ready to evacuate their homes?

6. What's the best way to cope with an emergency such as a heart attack?

## Grammar: Unreal conditional in the present

| Use the present unreal conditional to talk about a situation that is not true now. | If you **were** in an emergency situation, you **would know** what to do. (You're not in an emergency situation at the moment.) |
|---|---|
| Conditional sentences have two clauses: the condition clause and the result clause. | **Condition:** *if* + subject + past tense verb<br>**Result:** subject + *would* + base form of verb |
| The condition clause can be at the beginning or end of the sentence. | I **would bring** a lot of warm clothes **if** I **were** you.<br>**If** I **were** you, I **would bring** a lot of warm clothes. |
| When the verb *be* is in the condition clause, we always use *were*. (*Was* is only used informally.) | If the building **were** on fire, we **would** evacuate.<br>~~If it **was** on fire, we **wouldn't** panic.~~ |
| **Note:** Use a comma when the condition clause is at the beginning of a sentence. | |

**A** Match the conditions to the results.

1. If you fell from a high place, _____        a. a doctor would diagnose it.

2. If you planned for emergencies, _____        b. if you were struck by lightning.

3. You would die of thirst _____        c. you would be better prepared.

4. If you had a serious illness, _____        d. you would break your leg.

5. You would be electrocuted _____        e. if you were in the desert.

**B** 🔁 What would you do? Complete the sentences and then compare your ideas with your partner's ideas.

1. If I were bitten by a poisonous snake, I would _____

2. If this building were on fire, I would _____

3. If I were in a flood, I would _____

4. If I felt an earthquake happening, I would _____

5. If I had to buy supplies for a camping trip, I would _____

## Conversation

**A** 🔊 19 Close your book and listen to the conversation. What advice does Nathan give Isabel?

**Isabel:** Nathan, do you ever get worried?

**Nathan:** About what?

**Isabel:** Oh, you know—about things that can kill you.

**Nathan:** Sometimes I think about how we would get out of this apartment building if there were a fire.

**Isabel:** Right! Or what you would do if you were lost in the mountains after a plane crash!

**Nathan:** Well, that doesn't sound very likely.

**Isabel:** That's true, and I hope it never happens, but what if it did happen?

**Nathan:** Look, you can't worry about everything, but you can prepare for some things.

**Isabel:** Which things?

**Nathan:** Things that are more likely to happen, like fires or earthquakes.

**Isabel:** Good idea. Let's start by making an evacuation plan in case we need to get out of this building.

▲ Traffic caused by forest fire

**B** 🔁 Practice the conversation with a partner. Then switch roles and practice it again.

**C** 🔁 Make new conversations about the things you worry about.

**D** 🔁 **GOAL CHECK** ✓ **Talk about emergency situations**

Talk with a partner about emergency situations that are likely to happen where you live. What would you do in these situations?

▲ Students practicing martial arts

## Listening

**A** 🔊 **20** Listen to a radio call-in show. What situations did the callers survive?

Caller #1: _____          Caller #3: _____

Caller #2: _____

### Engage!

Did the callers on the radio show do the right thing? Is there anything you would do differently in those situations?

**B** 🔊 **20** Listen again. Circle the answers.

1. When was Caller #1 in an emergency situation?

   **a.** last week          **b.** last month          **c.** last year

2. Where was Caller #2 when his emergency occurred?

   **a.** at home          **b.** at work          **c.** at school

3. What was the result of Caller #3's emergency?

   **a.** cuts and bruises          **b.** serious injuries          **c.** a large payment

## Pronunciation: Reduced speech: *D'ya* and *didja*

### Notice

When people speak quickly, they sometimes shorten or reduce words. For example:
   Do you → *D'ya*
   Did you → *Didja*

**A** 🔊 **21** Listen and repeat.

| Full form | Reduced speech |
|---|---|
| 1. Do you know the answer? | 1. *D'ya* know the answer? |
| 2. Did you get the message? | 2. *Didja* get the message? |
| 3. Do you have a plan? | 3. *D'ya* have a plan? |
| 4. Did you take an aspirin? | 4. *Didja* take an aspirin? |

**B** 🔊 **22** Listen to the questions and circle the form you hear.

1.     full     reduced          4.     full     reduced
2.     full     reduced          5.     full     reduced
3.     full     reduced          6.     full     reduced

**C** ✐ Write two questions with *Do you . . .* ? and two with *Did you . . .* ? Then ask a partner your questions using reduced speech.

# Communication

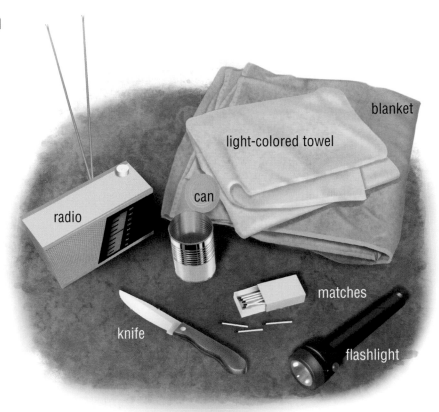

radio

can

light-colored towel

blanket

knife

matches

flashlight

**A** Talk about the survival situations in the box with a partner. What kinds of problems would you face in each situation?

> lost in a forest
> vehicle broken down in a desert
> trapped in a building after an earthquake

**B** Choose one of the survival situations from exercise **A.** Discuss with your partner how each of the items below could help you survive in an emergency. Then choose the three most useful items.

| | | |
|---|---|---|
| a blanket | a cell phone | a first-aid kit |
| water | a radio | matches |
| a knife | an empty can | a flashlight |
| a plastic trash bag | snack foods | a light-colored towel |

**C** Brainstorm ways in which the three items you chose in exercise **B** could help you to survive.

**D** **GOAL CHECK** ✓ **Evaluate survival methods**

Join another pair of students and compare the items you chose. Explain why each item you chose in exercise **B** would be very important in a survival situation.

## Language Expansion: Environmental conservation

**A** Read the article. Notice the words in blue.

New Zealand is doing something to protect its ocean species. The country has banned all types of fishing in 31 ocean reserves—areas devoted to the preservation of marine life.

When the first reserve was opened in 1977, many residents in the area were opposed to the idea. But when the fishing stopped, the ecosystem recovered quickly. The snapper returned to the area, and these predatory fish began to eat the sea urchins that had destroyed many ocean plants. As the ocean habitat was restored, endangered species increased in number.

Surprisingly, New Zealand's coastal reserves have also helped the fishing industry. Fish eggs and baby fish drift outside the reserves into surrounding areas where fishing is allowed. Today, commercial fishermen are some of the strongest defenders of the reserves.

▲ A New Zealand fur seal swims through kelp.

### Engage!

Do you think fishing or hunting should be banned where you live? What other ways can you think of to preserve plant and animal species?

**B** Fill in each blank with one of the words in blue.

1. Parts of the ocean where you can't go fishing are called _____.

2. _____ animals eat other animals.

3. When something is _____, it goes back to the way it was before.

4. A _____ is a certain kind of plant or animal.

5. When something is _____, it is prohibited by law.

6. _____ means keeping or maintaining something.

7. An _____ is plants and animals in a certain area.

8. An _____ species might become extinct.

## Grammar: *Wish* in the present

| | |
|---|---|
| We use *wish* when we want things to be different than they really are. | I **wish** I **didn't** have to get up early. (In reality, I do have to get up early.) |
| The verb after *wish* is in the past tense. | I **wish** the fish **were** protected. (They're not protected.)<br>I **wish** you **spoke** Russian. (You don't.) |
| After *wish*, the auxiliary verbs *can* or *will* change to *could* or *would*. | We **wish** you **could** come to our house.<br>I **wish** they **would** ban fishing here. |

**A** Fill in each blank with the correct form of the word in parentheses.

1. I wish I _____ (know) the answer, but I'm afraid I can't help you.

2. I wish I _____ (live) in New Zealand.

3. Akira wishes he _____ (can) do more to help wildlife.

4. I wish people _____ (not, kill) so many wild animals.

5. Many people wish they _____ (have) more money.

6. I wish my best friend _____ (be) here. I want to talk to her.

**B** Use the ideas below to tell your partner about things you wish were different than they are. Add two ideas of your own to share with the class.

Tigers and pandas are endangered.          People destroy animal habitats.

People kill elephants for their tusks.          _____

People catch sharks for shark fin soup.          _____

## Conversation

**A** 🔊 **23**   Close your book and listen to the conversation. In what ways do meerkats cooperate in order to survive?

**Andrew:** Do you ever wish you were an animal?

**Caleb:** Sure. Sometimes I wish I were a bird so I could fly.

**Andrew:** I wish I were a meerkat.

**Caleb:** A meerkat? What's that?

**Andrew:** It's an African animal. It survives by living in groups and cooperating.

**Caleb:** How do they cooperate?

**Andrew:** When there's a predator nearby, they make a warning sound. Then all the meerkats go into their holes.

**Caleb:** That sounds helpful. What else do they do?

**Andrew:** They babysit for each other. That way, the parents have a chance to find food.

**Caleb:** I see what you mean. They're a very social animal.

**Andrew:** Right, and if I were a meerkat, I wouldn't have to carry these boxes by myself. I could get some help from you!

**Caleb:** Oh, sorry. Can I give you a hand with those?

▲ Two meerkats guarding the group

**Real Language**

When you *give someone a hand*, you help them do some work.

**B** 🔄 Practice the conversation with a partner. Then switch roles and practice it again.

**C** 🔗 **GOAL CHECK** ✔ **Describe how animals survive**

Work in a group. Make a list of several animals and discuss some of the things these animals do to survive. Tell your group which animal you wish you were and why.

## Reading

**A** ↪ What happens at a survival school? Discuss with a partner. List three activities you think you will read about in the article.

_____

_____

_____

**B** Answer the following questions. If necessary, look back at the article.

1. Give two reasons people might want to visit southern Utah. _____

2. When did BOSS start teaching people to survive outdoors? _____

3. What materials do BOSS students use to make shelters? _____

4. What materials do BOSS students use to make a fire? _____

5. What kind of people can participate in BOSS courses? _____

6. What do BOSS students like about survival school? _____

**C** ↪ Tell a partner about the kind of challenges you enjoy. Then talk about a specific experience in your life that has increased your confidence.

▲ Lighting dry tinder by blowing on ember

Boulder, Utah, USA

# SURVIVAL SCHOOL

● Boulder, Utah

**Big Bend in Colorado River, near Lake Powell, Utah, Arizona, USA**

_purify_ to make safe to drink **brush** dry plants and sticks used for burning
_endure_ to continue with an activity over a long period of time
_canyon_ a narrow, steep area between two mountains
_enthusiast_ a person who is very interested in an activity or subject

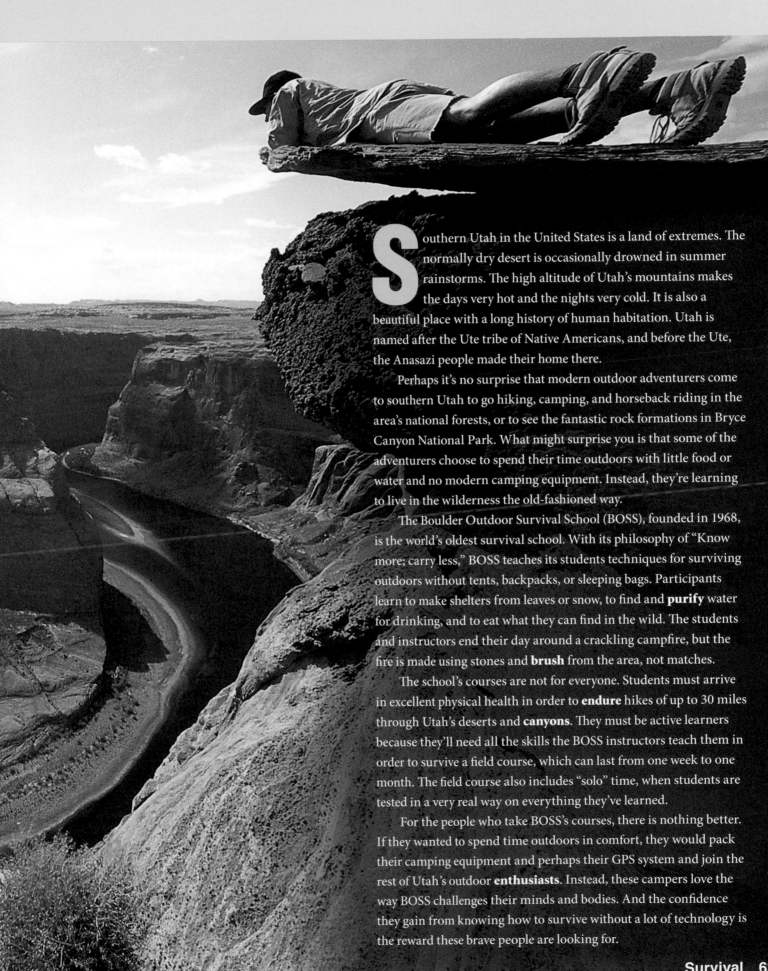

Southern Utah in the United States is a land of extremes. The normally dry desert is occasionally drowned in summer rainstorms. The high altitude of Utah's mountains makes the days very hot and the nights very cold. It is also a beautiful place with a long history of human habitation. Utah is named after the Ute tribe of Native Americans, and before the Ute, the Anasazi people made their home there.

Perhaps it's no surprise that modern outdoor adventurers come to southern Utah to go hiking, camping, and horseback riding in the area's national forests, or to see the fantastic rock formations in Bryce Canyon National Park. What might surprise you is that some of the adventurers choose to spend their time outdoors with little food or water and no modern camping equipment. Instead, they're learning to live in the wilderness the old-fashioned way.

The Boulder Outdoor Survival School (BOSS), founded in 1968, is the world's oldest survival school. With its philosophy of "Know more; carry less," BOSS teaches its students techniques for surviving outdoors without tents, backpacks, or sleeping bags. Participants learn to make shelters from leaves or snow, to find and **purify** water for drinking, and to eat what they can find in the wild. The students and instructors end their day around a crackling campfire, but the fire is made using stones and **brush** from the area, not matches.

The school's courses are not for everyone. Students must arrive in excellent physical health in order to **endure** hikes of up to 30 miles through Utah's deserts and **canyons**. They must be active learners because they'll need all the skills the BOSS instructors teach them in order to survive a field course, which can last from one week to one month. The field course also includes "solo" time, when students are tested in a very real way on everything they've learned.

For the people who take BOSS's courses, there is nothing better. If they wanted to spend time outdoors in comfort, they would pack their camping equipment and perhaps their GPS system and join the rest of Utah's outdoor **enthusiasts**. Instead, these campers love the way BOSS challenges their minds and bodies. And the confidence they gain from knowing how to survive without a lot of technology is the reward these brave people are looking for.

Survival school activity

## Communication

**A** 🔁 Think of a place in your country where a survival school would work well. Make a list of several reasons why it would be a good place for a survival school. Then list things the students would learn and experience.

**B** 👥 Get together with another pair of students and compare your lists. Try to agree on which location would be the best for a survival school.

> **Compound Sentences**
>
> Connect clauses and show relationships between ideas with *and*, *or*, *but*, and *so*.
>
> *Students must survive alone in the forest, **but** they have all the supplies they need, **so** they will be safe.*

## Writing

**A** Follow the directions below.

1. Choose one of the locations you discussed in the Communication exercise and write two paragraphs for an advertising brochure.

2. In the first paragraph, describe the place and explain why it's a good location.

3. In the second paragraph, describe the things students do and learn at the school. Use compound sentences if possible.

**B** 🔁 Exchange brochures with a partner and answer the questions. Does the information in the first paragraph help you to imagine the place? Does the information in the second paragraph make the school sound interesting? Does your partner use compound sentences to show relationships between ideas?

**C** 🔁 **GOAL CHECK** ✔ **Write a brochure**

Tell your partner which parts of his or her brochure you like the most. Suggest other details your partner could add.

## Before You Watch

**A** Chinchero, Peru, is a small village in the Andes Mountains. Underline the ways you think the Chinchero villagers might make their living.

herding animals such as sheep          selling local crafts to tourists
raising crops such as potatoes         managing a large discount store
working in big office buildings        teaching at local schools

## While You Watch

**A** ▶ Circle **T** for *true* and **F** for *false*. Make the false statements true.

1. Sheep are raised for their wool in Chinchero.          T     F

2. Many of the men in Chinchero are farmers.              T     F

3. Many of the women in Chinchero weave textiles.         T     F

4. Farming is the only way to make money in Chinchero.    T     F

5. Older women teach weaving to younger women.            T     F

**B** ▶ Watch the video again and take brief notes to answer these questions:

1. How does weaving contribute to economic survival in Chinchero?

2. How does weaving contribute to cultural survival in Chinchero?

## After You Watch / Communication

**A** 🔁 Design a tourism brochure with a brief description of traditional products made where you live.

**B** 👥 You are members of the Center for Traditional Textiles cooperative. Brainstorm a list of new ways to market and sell products.

# Art

Guggenheim Museum Bilbao
in Bilbao, Spain

**Look at the photo, answer the questions:**

**1** What is this a picture of? Where is it?

**2** Do you like it? Why or why not?

**UNIT 6 GOALS**

**1.** Report what another person said

**2.** Express your opinions about a piece of art

**3.** Describe your favorite artists and their art

**4.** Talk about public art

## Vocabulary

**A** Read the article. Notice the words in blue.

▲ Botero sculpture in Ramble del Ravel, Barcelona, Spain

Public art is an enjoyable part of daily life in Singapore. Large sculptures and colorful paintings called murals can be found in parks, shopping centers, and along this island nation's coastlines. The artistic styles range from quite realistic to completely abstract.

Some of the art is by well-known artists from other countries, including Fernando Botero of Colombia. His sculpture of a bird represents peace and optimism. Sculptures by Singaporean artist Chong Fah Cheong depict people living and working in traditional ways along the Singapore River. Since Chong didn't study art formally, he developed his techniques for sculpting metal on his own.

Public art in Singapore is supported by businesses and government, and whether or not people are aware of it, the art contributes to a high quality of life for people in this vibrant and culturally diverse city.

**B** Write the words in blue next to their meanings in your notebook.

1. methods or procedures
2. similar to real life
3. to paint or draw a person or a thing
4. having a lot of variety
5. is a symbol for something
6. art made from solid materials
7. not a concrete thing
8. knowing that something exists
9. pictures on a flat surface
10. kinds of artistic design

## Grammar: Reported speech

| | |
|---|---|
| Use reported speech to say what another person said. The word *that* is optional. | "I'm an artist." **Meg said (that) she was an artist.** |
| The verb in reported speech usually changes: 1) from present to past 2) from past to past perfect | "I **paint** every day." He said that he **painted** every day. "I **won** an award." She said she **had won** an award. |
| Pronouns usually change in reported speech. | "**We** saw some sculptures downtown." Tom told me **they** had seen some sculptures downtown. |
| Other words can also change in reported speech. | "I'm returning the books **tomorrow**." She said that she was returning the books **the next day**. |

**A** Read what Andy Chao, Young Artist of the Year, said in an interview. Write his statements in reported speech.

1. "I make sculptures with glass and metal."  He said he _____

2. "My newest sculpture is 10 meters tall." _____

3. "I'm flying to Germany tomorrow." _____

4. "I don't know how long I'll stay in Berlin." _____

5. "I'm going to show my work in a famous gallery." _____

6. "I can't talk about my next sculpture." _____

**B** 🗣 Think about the last time you talked to your best friend on the phone. Use reported speech to tell your partner about the conversation.

## Conversation

**A** 🔊 24 Listen to the conversation with your book closed. What did Jennie's brother say about the paintings?

**Mia:** Hi, Jennie. What did you do over the weekend?

**Jennie:** Nothing special on Saturday, but on Sunday I went to the student painting show at the art institute.

**Mia:** You're kidding! I thought you didn't like art very much.

**Jennie:** Not usually, but my brother told me about the show. He said the paintings were amazing.

**Mia:** So, what did you think of them?

**Jennie:** I thought they were great! A lot of them were realistic, with the most wonderful details.

**Mia:** Did you meet any of the artists?

**Jennie:** Yes, I met one of them. She told me her painting represented energy. It was just three blue circles!

**Mia:** That sounds pretty abstract.

**B** 🗣 Practice the conversation with a partner. Then make new conversations about the picture on the right.

**C** 🗣 **GOAL CHECK** ✔ **Report what another person said**

What did your partner say about the picture in exercise **B**? Tell a new partner. Use reported speech.

> Carmen said she was having a very bad day.

> Really? What happened?

**Real Language**

*You're kidding!* is an informal expression that shows you're surprised or don't believe what the other person said.

▲ sculpture garden

## Listening

**A**  Look at these paintings. Describe them to a partner.

> Painting A is abstract, but I think it represents feelings.

a.

b.

d.

c.

e.

**B** 🔊 25 You are going to hear conversations in a museum about three of these paintings. Write the letter of the painting the people are talking about.

Conversation 1: _____   Conversation 2: _____   Conversation 3: _____

**C** 🔊 25 Listen to the conversations again. What did the people say about the paintings? Circle the correct answer.

| | |
|---|---|
| **Conversation 1** | 1. The man said the painting was (interesting/boring). <br> 2. The woman said the painting was (peaceful/beautiful). |
| **Conversation 2** | 3. The man said the painting was (abstract/dramatic). <br> 4. The woman said the painting was just colored (lines/shapes). |
| **Conversation 3** | 5. The man said the scene in the painting was (happy/realistic). <br> 6. The woman said the painting was (bright/large). |

**D** 🔁 Do you agree with the man's ideas about the paintings? Explain your answers to a partner.

## Pronunciation: Thought groups

When speaking, we usually divide long sentences into phrases called "thought groups." These groups are on one topic or are part of one grammatical structure. A thought group usually 1) has one focus word, and 2) ends with a falling intonation and sometimes a slight pause.

**A** 🔊 26 Listen and repeat these sentences. Notice the thought groups.

1. Ruth said | that abstract sculptures | were her favorite | kind of art.

2. The realistic sculpture | of children going swimming | is called *The First Generation*.

3. "Let's come back tomorrow," | said Lee, | "when the museum | is less crowded."

4. In the evening, | we like to walk | along the river.

5. Moneera said, | "If you like this painting, | you can buy a print | from the gift shop."

6. The instructor said | we had done well | on the quiz, | which made us happy.

**B** 🔗 With a partner, underline the focus word in each phrase.

1. I really like the painting | because it represents freedom.

2. Johan told Maria | she could see the sculptures | in McKinley Park.

3. "In a moment," | said Mr. Wong, | "we'll go upstairs | to see the paintings."

4. He said | we were leaving | in an hour.

5. I didn't realize | that most of her techniques | were developed in Malaysia.

6. Cindy said, | "If we don't leave soon, | we'll be late | for the concert."

**C** 🔗 🔊 27 Listen to the sentences from exercise **B** and check your answers. Then practice saying the sentences with your partner.

## Communication

**A** 👥 Discuss the paintings on the previous page and pick the best one to hang in each of these places.

- a very expensive restaurant
- the living room of a family apartment
- the waiting room in a hospital
- the office of a company president

**B** 👥 Explain your decisions to the class. Use thought groups to divide your longer sentences.

**C** 🔗 **GOAL CHECK** ✔ **Express your opinions about a piece of art**

Which of the paintings do you like the least? Explain your opinion to a partner.

> **Content words** have a specific meaning, not just a grammatical function. They include:
>
> **nouns**          **verbs**
>
>     **question words**
>
> **adjectives**     **adverbs**
>
> The **focus word,** often the last content word in a sentence or phrase, receives extra emphasis.

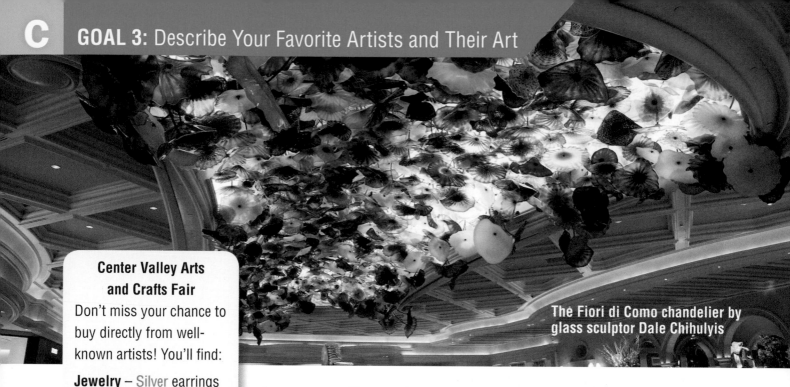

The Fiori di Como chandelier by glass sculptor Dale Chihulyis

## Language Expansion: Art materials

**A** Read the advertisement and notice the words in blue.

**B** Write each word in blue next to its definition. Use a dictionary to help you.

1. _____ semi-hard material from trees
2. _____ material made at high temperatures
3. _____ any kind of woven cloth
4. _____ expensive, light-colored metal
5. _____ soft material made from earth and water
6. _____ material made from animal skin
7. _____ dark-colored, brown metal
8. _____ hard material found in the ground

**C** What are some traditional crafts from your country? What are they made of?

## Grammar: Subject adjective clauses

| | |
|---|---|
| You can meet <u>people</u>. (<u>They</u> make traditional crafts.) <br> You'll find <u>presents</u>. (<u>They</u> are perfect for all your friends.) <br> An <u>artist</u> has strong hands. (<u>He</u> works with clay.) | You can meet people **who make traditional crafts**. <br> You'll find **presents that are perfect for all your friends**. <br> An artist **who works with clay has strong hands**. |

\* An adjective clause modifies (gives more information about) a noun. It comes after the noun.
\* Use *who* in adjective clauses about people, to replace *he, she,* or *they.*
\* Use *that* in adjective clauses about things, to replace *it* or *they.* We can use *which* instead of *that* in more formal sentences.

**A** Write sentences with adjective clauses about these artists' works. Use the information in the box.

1. A painter *is a person who paints pictures.* _____
2. A poet _____
3. A songwriter _____
4. A sculptor _____
5. An author _____
6. A director _____

| |
|---|
| paint pictures |
| write books |
| make movies |
| write poems |
| carve statues |
| write pop songs |

**B** Write sentences with subject adjective clauses that modify the underlined word.

1. I bought a <u>pot</u>. It was made in Korea. *I bought a pot that was made in Korea.* _____
2. Jenna has two <u>brothers</u>. They are artists. _____
3. The <u>woman</u> is from Brazil. She lives next door. _____
4. <u>Everyone</u> learned a lot. They took the class. _____
5. Where is the <u>book</u>? It was on the table. _____
6. I don't like those <u>paintings</u>. They are hard to understand. _____

## Conversation

**A** 🔊 28 Listen to the conversation with your book closed. What kind of crafts does Carrie like?

**Emily:** Where did you get that jacket, Carrie? It's really beautiful!

**Carrie:** Thank you! I bought it in the Fair Trade store. They have crafts from all different countries, and they pay the artists a fair price.

**Emily:** Sounds interesting. What else do they have there?

**Carrie:** Oh, lots of cool things! I also bought some coffee cups from Mexico, and I've been using them every day. I really like crafts that are useful.

**Emily:** Do you? For me, the most important thing is the style. I want crafts that look handmade—not like they came from a machine.

**Carrie:** Well, I'm sure you can find something you like there.

**Emily:** Next time you go, I'd like to go along.

**B** 🔄 Practice the conversation with a partner. Then make new conversations about these things. Use your own opinions.

| paintings | cooking utensils | clothes |
|---|---|---|

> **I like clothes that don't cost too much!**

**C** 🔄 **GOAL CHECK** ✓ **Describe your favorite artists and their art**

Work with a partner. Take turns describing your favorite artists and their creations. Use subject adjective clauses in your descriptions.

## Reading

**A** List all of the places where you can see art in your city. What can you see in each place?

**B** Read the article. Match the sentence parts to show the reasons.

1. The murals are in bad condition ___

2. Artists didn't maintain the murals ___

3. Artists in L.A. started painting murals ___

4. Judith Baca's mural is special ___

5. Kent Twitchell calls his mural a gateway ___

6. Many artists like murals ___

a. because it is unusually long.

b. because of dirty air and hot weather.

c. because people drive through it.

d. because so many people see them.

e. because it was difficult and dangerous.

f. because they liked the work of Mexican artists.

**C** 🔁 Discuss these questions with a partner.

1. Describe the mural in the picture. What do you think it represents?

2. What is your opinion of this mural? Explain your answers.

3. Would murals like this be popular in your city? Why or why not?

> People like art that makes them smile!

Los Angeles, California, USA

SAVING A CITY'S

**A**voiding L.A.'s traffic jams may be impossible, but the city's colorful highway murals can brighten even the worst commute. Paintings that depict famous people and historical scenes cover office buildings and highway walls all across the city. With a collection of more than 2,000 murals, Los Angeles is the unofficial mural capital of the world.

But a combination of graffiti, pollution, and hot sun has left many L.A. murals in terrible condition. In the past, experts say, little attention was given to caring for public art. Artists were even expected to maintain their own works—not an easy task with cars racing by on the highway! Now the city is beginning a huge project

# PUBLIC ART

to **restore** its murals. So far, 16 walls have been selected, and more may be added later.

Until about 1960, public murals in Los Angeles were rare. But in the '60s and '70s, young L.A. artists began to study early 20th-century Mexican mural painting. Soon, the young artists' own murals became a symbol of the city's cultural diversity.

The most famous mural in the city is Judith Baca's "The Great Wall," a 13-foot-high (4-meter-high) painting that runs for half a mile (0.8 kilometer) in North Hollywood. The mural represents the history of different **ethnic groups** in California. It took eight years to complete, with 400 teenagers painting the designs, and is probably the longest mural in the world.

One of the murals that will be restored is Kent Twitchell's "Seventh Street Altarpiece," which he painted for the Los Angeles Olympics in 1984. This **striking** work depicts two people facing each other on opposite sides of the highway near downtown Los Angeles. "It was meant as a kind of **gateway** through which the traveler to L.A. must drive," said Twitchell. "The open hands represent peace." Artists often call murals *the people's art*. Along a busy highway or hidden in a quiet neighborhood, murals can reach people who might never pay money to see fine art in a museum.

*restore* return to original condition   *ethnic groups* people from a certain culture
*striking* visually impressive   *gateway* opening in a wall or fence

▲ *Nutmeg and Mace* by Kumari Nahappan

> We want a sculpture that will represent the children of this community.

> It will be in the park which is near the elementary school.

## Communication

**A** 👥 Imagine your group is in charge of planning a new piece of public art for the area near your school. Discuss the questions.

1. What kind of art will you have: a mural, sculpture, stained glass window, or something else?

2. Where will the art be located, and why is it a good location for the art?

**B** 👥 Draw a picture of the public art piece your group imagined in exercise **A**. Present your group's ideas to the class, using adjective clauses to describe the art and location.

## Writing

**A** Write one or two paragraphs about a work of public art that you like. Describe what the art looks like, what it represents, and explain why you like it.

**B** 🔄 Exchange your writing with a partner. Read your partner's writing carefully.

**C** 👥 | **GOAL CHECK** ✔ **Talk about public art**

Use reported speech to tell another pair of students what your partner wrote about in his or her paragraph.

> My partner wrote about the mural on Main Street. She said it is in a realistic style, and that it represented the history of exploration.

### Writing Strategy

Provide plenty of details to help the reader imagine the thing you're describing.

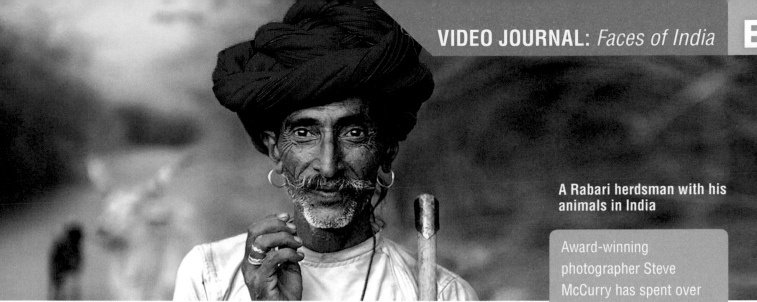

**A Rabari herdsman with his animals in India**

Award-winning photographer Steve McCurry has spent over 30 years traveling the world and taking pictures of the people he meets. He has traveled to India many times and documented that country's rich cultural diversity. In this video, McCurry discusses the people and culture of Rajasthan—a state in northern India.

## Before You Watch

**A** Read about National Geographic photographer Steve McCurry. What do you think are the positive aspects of working as a photographer?

**B** 🔁 Discuss the questions with a partner.

1. Do you enjoy photographing people? Why or why not?

2. What must a photographer do in order to take good pictures of people?

## While You Watch

**A** Take notes on things you see in the video.

1. The land in Rajasthan _____ .

2. Making a living in Rajasthan _____ .

3. Clothing in Rajasthan _____ .

4. McCurry's behavior _____ .

**B** Fill in the blanks with words you hear in the video.

1. McCurry's first job after college was working for _____ .

2. The state of Rajasthan is on India's border with _____ .

3. McCurry says going to Rajasthan is like going to another _____ .

4. McCurry thinks it's the _____ that tells a story, not the eyes or any one particular feature.

## After You Watch / Communication

**A** 🔁 Discuss the quotation with your classmates. What do you think McCurry means?

*There's no place in the world that has the depth of culture like India.*

# TED TALKS

**Amit Sood** Head, Google Art Project; Group Marketing Manager for Google

## BUILDING A MUSEUM OF MUSEUMS ON THE WEB

## Before You Watch

**A** 🔄 Look at the picture and answer the questions with a partner.

1. Where is this person? What is he doing?

2. Why do people go to museums?

3. When was the last time you went to a museum? What did you see there?

**B** In his TED Talk, Amit Sood describes a very unusual museum. Here are some words you will hear in his TED Talk. Complete the paragraph with the correct word. Not all words will be used.

> **access** *n.* a way of being able to use or get something
> **annotate** *v.* to add notes or comments to (a text, book, drawing, etc.)
> **brushstrokes** *n.* the paint left on a painting by a movement of the artist's brush
> **cracks** *n.* thin lines in the surface of something that is broken but not separated into pieces
> **launch** *v.* to offer or sell (something) for the first time
> **negotiations** *n.* formal discussions between people who are trying to reach an agreement

When Amit Sood was growing up in India, he didn't have (1) _____ to museums. Now, he works at Google, where he has just (2) _____ a project that will bring museums to people everywhere. Sood has been in (3) _____ with some of the most important museums in the

Amit Sood's idea worth spreading is that we should all have access to the world's best museums and artwork at any time of the day or night. Technology can let us have that. Watch Sood's full TED Talk on TED.com.

world to get their art online. The Google Art Project allows you to view art even closer than you can in real life—you can see the artist's (4) _____ and the (5)_____ that have developed after many years. Even more interesting is the ability to (6) _____ the images with your own ideas and share it with your friends. It's a completely new way of looking at art.

**C** Look at the pictures on the next page. Check (✓) the information that you predict you will hear in the TED Talk.

_____ 1. It was very expensive to create the Google Art Project.

_____ 2. There are many images on the Google Art Project Web site.

_____ 3. If you have a computer, you have access to museum collections around the world.

## While You Watch

**A** ▶ Watch the TED Talk. Circle the main idea.

1. It is important for people to see as much art as possible.

2. Amit Sood didn't go to many museums when he was growing up in India.

3. Sood developed the Google Art Project to make art accessible through technology.

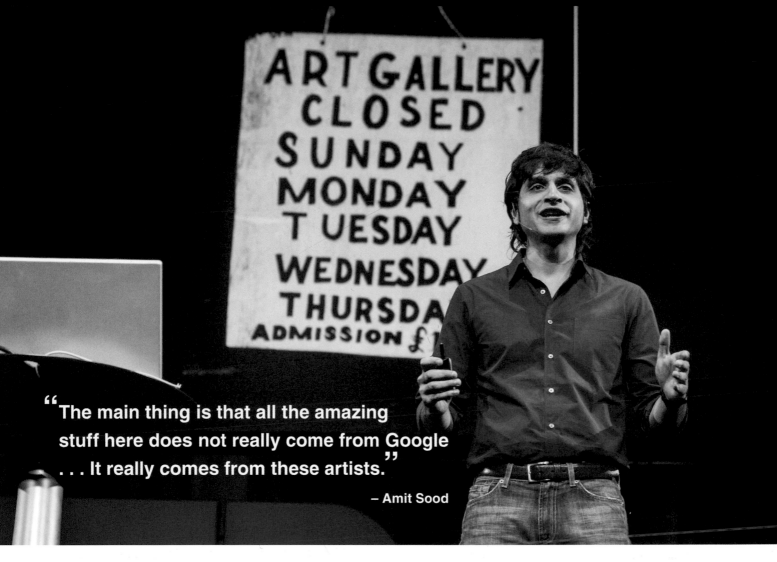

> "The main thing is that all the amazing stuff here does not really come from Google . . . It really comes from these artists."
>
> – Amit Sood

**B** ▶ The photos below relate to the ideas in the TED Talk. Watch the talk again and write the letter of the caption under the correct photo.

**a.** Many people lack access to museums.

**b.** The Google Art site contains artwork from more than 300 museums.

**c.** You can create collections of images and share them with your friends.

**d.** Using Google Art, it's possible to view the details of the paintings.

1. ___

2. ___

3. ___

4. ___

**Challenge!** ↻ What other cultural resources do you think should be available on the Internet? Share your ideas with a partner.

# TEDTALKS

**Amit Sood** Head, Google Art Project; Group Marketing Manager for Google

## BUILDING A MUSEUM OF MUSEUMS ON THE WEB

**Tour of Chinese art exhibition**

## After You Watch

**A** Complete the summary with the words in the box.

> artwork   computer   goal   negotiate   study

The Google Art Project has a unique (1) _____ to share the world's greatest (2) _____ on the Internet. Amit Sood and his team (3) _____ with important museums in order to gain access to their works. If you have a (4) _____, you can move around in a museum, (5) _____ the art, and save the paintings and sculptures you like best.

**B** Match the phrases to complete sentences from the TED Talk.

**Cause**

1. _____ The Google Art Project was developed
2. _____ The project began with
3. _____ You can look at the images
4. _____ Some images can contain
5. _____ When you find an image you like,

**Effect**

a. as many as 10 billion pixels.
b. you can save it or share it.
c. 17 museums in 9 countries.
d. in 18 months.
e. at normal size or close up.

**C** Read the statements below. Circle the ones that paraphrase Amit Sood's ideas.

1. I wanted to make it possible for many people to see the art in these museums.

2. It is necessary for users to understand that it was difficult and expensive to create the Google Art Project.

3. One of my favorite parts of the project is seeing the details of the paintings.

4. The most important thing about the Google Art Project is the artists themselves. The technology is amazing, but not as amazing as the art itself.

## Project

**A** Look at the list of cultural resources. Circle the two that are most important in your life.

> archaeological sites    architecture    public art    museums    ballet
> community festivals    orchestra    theater    cinema

**B** Compare your choices in exercise **A** with a partner. What reasons do they give for their choices? Would you change any of your choices as a result?

**C** Work with a group. Choose three cultural resources in your city or country that you want to share with the world on the Internet. Use the table to organize your ideas.

| Cultural Resource | Information to Include | Images |
|---|---|---|
|  |  |  |
|  |  |  |

**Research Strategy**

Looking for additional information

It's often helpful to begin researching a subject at its official Web site. Click on related links to obtain more information.

**Challenge!** Although Amit Sood is the head of the Google Art Project, he didn't create it alone. Go to his speaker profile on TED.com and read more about the team's inspiration for the project. In addition to technology know-how, what other kinds of skills do you think the team members needed to create their virtual museum?

# Getting Around

Bullet train at station

**Look at the photo, answer the questions:**

**1** Which form of transportation is the most important in your country now?

**2** Which will be the most important in the future?

**UNIT 7 GOALS**

1. Talk about new developments

2. Discuss choices in transportation

3. Use English to get around

4. Make recommendations for improving transportation

▲ A view of video screens on the backs of seats of an airplane

## Vocabulary

**A** ⚡ Read the article. Which of these ideas do you think will be successful?

**The Future of Flying**
- Today, the largest airplanes carry over 850 passengers, and the size of planes will only increase. New airplanes have been designed that will carry up to 900 people.
- Huge aircrafts are being planned that will carry vehicles and other goods across the ocean. They will fly only seven meters above the water at a low speed.
- Very small planes called "Personal Air Vehicles" are also in the works and may someday take you, and perhaps a few of your friends, directly to your destination.
- Quieter and more efficient planes are being developed as well, and new materials and designs will reduce their use of fuel.
- Many modern airplanes are actually flown by computers between takeoff and landing. In the future, some planes won't have a pilot at all!

**B** Write the words in blue next to their meanings.

1. _____ place you are going to

2. _____ how fast something moves

3. _____ without stopping or changing direction

4. _____ substance burned to give power

5. _____ means of transportation, such as cars

6. _____ to make smaller

7. _____ not using too much time or energy

8. _____ people who are traveling in a vehicle

## Grammar: Passive voice with the present continuous and present perfect tenses

| | |
|---|---|
| The passive voice can be used with any verb tense. Use the passive with the present continuous to talk about things that are in progress now. | *am/is/are* + *being* + past participle<br>Larger planes **are being developed.**<br>The technology **is being tested** now. |
| Use the passive with the present perfect to talk about things in the past that have an effect on the present. | *have/has* + *been* + past participle<br>New types of planes **have been designed.**<br>Computers **have been used** for decades. |

**A** Complete the paragraph with the passive present perfect of the verb.

Many solo flights around the world (1) _____ (make) since the first one in 1933. However, such a flight (2) _____ (complete) only once by a person born in Jamaica. It happened in 2007, when Barrington Irving was only 23 years old. Since then, Irving has been teaching children about building and piloting airplanes, and he (3) _____ (name) one of National Geographic's Emerging Explorers. Around the world, many young people (4) _____ (inspire) by people such as Irving who are able to share themselves and their careers and motivate others to do great things.

**B** Complete the article with the passive present continuous of the verb.

**Cars for Tomorrow**

New discoveries (1) _are being made_ (make) every day. Automobiles are changing very fast. Already, energy-efficient cars (2) _____ (sell) in many countries. Very small, light cars for one person (3) _____ (design). Cars that run on hydrogen (4) _____ (test), and electric vehicles (5) _____ (use) in some cities. More corn (6) _____ (grow) to make ethanol for fuel.

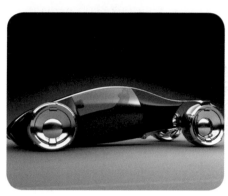

## Conversation

**A** 🔊 2 Listen to the conversation with your book closed. What kind of car will Jake get next month?

**Cassie:** The price of gas is getting so high. I think I'm going to get rid of my car and take the bus.

**Jake:** Not me! I'm getting a new car next month. It's a hybrid.

**Cassie:** You mean, one of those electric cars?

**Jake:** Not exactly. It uses both electricity and gasoline.

**Cassie:** Well, I don't like to be the first person to try something new. New technology always has a lot of problems.

**Jake:** That's not always true. Besides, electric cars have been used for a long time.

**Cassie:** Well, I'd like to see your hybrid car when you get it. Will you take me for a ride?

**Jake:** Sure! And maybe I'll even let you drive it.

**B** ⚡ Practice the conversation. Then talk about these new kinds of cars.

**C** ⚡ **GOAL CHECK** ✔ **Talk about new developments**

Tell your partner about ways transportation is changing in your part of the world.

## Listening

**A** 🔁 Discuss these questions with a partner. What are some famous cities with subways? Have you ever used a subway? What are some advantages and disadvantages of subways?

**B** 🔊 3 You will hear a radio program about things from the past discovered while building subways. Listen and write the name of each city and the discovery that was made there.

| City: _____ | City: _____ | City: _____ |
|---|---|---|
| Discovery: _____ | Discovery: _____ | Discovery: _____ |
| Year of discovery: _____ | Year of discovery: _____ | Year of discovery: _____ |
| They decided to: _____ _____ _____ | They decided to: _____ _____ _____ | They decided to: _____ _____ _____ |

**C** 🔊 3 Listen again and fill in the rest of the information in the chart.

**D** 🔁 Discuss these questions with a partner.

1. Do you think it's important to preserve archaeological discoveries when roads and subways are being built? Explain.

2. What are some other ways the construction of transportation systems might impact a city or a neighborhood?

## Pronunciation: Reduced *are*

**A** 🔊 4 The word *are* can sound like /ə/ in the middle of a sentence. Notice the pronunciation of *are* in the sentences below.

The buses **are** crowded.          Cars **are** parked on the street.

▲ Airport terminal hall

**B** 🔁 Read these sentences, paying attention to the pronunciation of *are*.

1. Those books are really funny.
2. How much are the tickets?
3. Those computers are made in China.
4. People are talking about him.
5. Cheaper cars are being sold.
6. Where are my keys?

## Communication

**A** Read about the situation.

### Airport Construction Delayed

Lomeria is a large city in a developing country. The airport in Lomeria is old and too small for many kinds of airplanes. Because of this, Lomeria is building a new airport. Now the terminal is being built, and an ancient city from 2,000 years ago has been uncovered by workers. Construction has stopped until the city government decides what to do. People in the neighborhood don't want a new airport. They say it will cause noise and pollution. Other people say the airport is necessary for the many tourists who come to Lomeria to experience its history and culture.

**B** 🔁 You are members of the Lomeria City Council. Add one more idea to the plans below. Then decide which plan is the best. Write two or three sentences to explain why your plan is the best one for Lomeria.

**Plan 1:**   Continue building the new airport. Don't change the plan.
**Plan 2:**   Build a smaller airport in the same place and preserve one part of the ancient city.
**Plan 3:**   Stop construction and use the money to preserve the ancient city.
**Plan 4:**   Stop construction and try to get more money to build a new airport in a different place.

**Plan 5:** _____

**C** 👥 **GOAL CHECK** ✔ **Discuss choices in transportation**

As a group, role-play a meeting about the airport problem. Make sure everyone explains his or her plan. Agree on the best plan.

Bus Rapid Transit, Curitiba, Brazil

## Language Expansion: Public transportation

**A** Read the article and notice the words in blue.

### Buses for the Future

The Bus Rapid Transit system of Curitiba, Brazil is famous for its convenience and design. Buses for up to 300 people travel all around the city. Passengers board the buses from comfortable glass *tube stations*. If they don't have a pass or a ticket, they pay their fare in the station, so everyone gets on the bus quickly when it arrives. They can transfer to another route without paying again. Where different bus routes connect, there are comfortable terminals with small shops and restrooms. The system is efficient, and it's very popular with the people of Curitiba.

**B** Discuss the questions with a partner. Use the words in blue from exercise **A.**

1. What are three ways to pay your fare on the Bus Rapid Transit system?
2. Where can people wait when they transfer from one route to another?
3. How do people in Curitiba feel about the bus system?
4. How do you feel about the public transportation where you live?

## Grammar: Indirect questions

| | |
|---|---|
| Indirect questions are inside statements or other questions. Use indirect questions to be more polite. | Do you know **if the bus stops** here? <br> Could you please tell me **how much the tickets cost**? |
| Use statement word order with indirect questions. Use *if* or *whether* in indirect *yes/no* questions. | Could you tell me **how long it takes** to get downtown? <br> Do you know **if/whether the train will be** on time? |

**A** Match the questions beginnings to their endings.

1. Do you know whether _____
2. Could you please tell _____
3. I'd like to know _____
4. Can you tell me where I can transfer _____
5. Do you know where _____

a. the train station is?
b. from Route 12 to Route 31?
c. me how much the fare is?
d. the flight from Brasilia has arrived yet?
e. if the terminal is open late at night.

**B** In your notebook, write polite indirect questions.

1. Does this train go to Central Station? (Do you know...)
2. What time does the next flight leave? (Can you tell me...)
3. Is there a subway station near here? (Could you please tell me...)
4. How much does a round-trip ticket cost? (I'd like to know...)
5. Where is the restroom? (Do you know...)

▲ Girl at ticket machine in Shibuya, Tokyo

## Conversation

**A** 🔊 **5** Luis is in a subway station in Tokyo. Listen to the conversation with your book closed. Where does he want to go?

**Luis:** Excuse me. Do you speak English?
**Yuki:** Yes, a little.
**Luis:** Could you please tell me how to get to the Imperial Palace Garden?
**Yuki:** From here, you take the Tozai subway line to Hibiya Station. Then you walk for about five minutes.
**Luis:** And can you tell me where I can buy a ticket?
**Yuki:** You get them from that machine. Let's see ... the fare is 250 yen. You put your money in here and push this button.
**Luis:** Great! Oh, one more question—do you know where I board the train?
**Yuki:** Just go down those stairs and you'll see a sign that says Tozai Line. It's in English.
**Luis:** Thanks for your help!
**Yuki:** You're welcome.

**B** 💬 Practice the conversation. Then switch roles and practice it again.

**C** 💬 **GOAL CHECK** ✔ **Use English to get around**

Make new conversations with a partner about how to get to places in your city.

> **Real Language**
>
> We often start a conversation with a stranger by saying *Excuse me,... Pardon me, ... I'm sorry to bother you, but ...*

> You take bus number 7 to the **university, and then transfer to ...**

## Reading

**A** 🔁 Discuss these questions with a partner.

1. What kinds of transportation did your city have 50 years ago?

2. Are those kinds of transportation still used today? Why or why not?

**B** Quickly skim the article. For each paragraph below, write **P** if it contains *positive* ideas about the topic or **N** if it contains *negative* ideas.

a. _____ Paragraph 2

b. _____ Paragraph 3

c. _____ Paragraph 4

**C** Circle **T** for *true* and **F** for *false*. Correct the false statements in your notebook.

1. Rickshaws are a traditional form of transportation in Kolkata.  **T  F**

2. The men who pull the rickshaws earn a lot of money.  **T  F**

3. Rickshaws can be used in parts of the city where buses can't drive.  **T  F**

4. Rickshaws are mostly used by wealthy people.  **T  F**

5. Rickshaws are a problem in heavy traffic.  **T  F**

6. The government is trying to increase the number of rickshaws.  **T  F**

7. There are programs now to help the rickshaw pullers get new jobs.  **T  F**

### Word Focus

**aging** = in the process of getting older

**narrow** = not wide

**crawling** = moving very slowly

Kolkata, India
# THE RICKSHAWS OF KOLKATA

Human-powered rickshaws first appeared in Kolkata, India a century ago, and about 6,000 of them still roll through the streets today. Most of the men who pull the rickshaws are poor, **aging** migrants from the countryside. Their vehicles are not being made any more, and as the parts wear out, they cannot be replaced. It appears that the days of the rickshaw are nearing their end in Kolkata.

Rickshaws are an important form of transportation in this city of nearly 15 million people. They are cheap and convenient. Poor and middle-class residents rely on rickshaws to move through **narrow** lanes in areas of the central city that are not served by public transportation. Families often pay a rickshaw puller to take their children to and from school.

Rickshaws also provide delivery service for hotels, shops, and homes around the city, carrying everything from food for 500 wedding guests to live chickens. Ladies on shopping trips depend on rickshaw pullers to wait while they make several stops before returning home. Some people even use a rickshaw instead of an ambulance!

Despite their usefulness, rickshaw pullers usually live in extreme poverty. Most of them are homeless. Some sleep in a *dera*, or rickshaw garage; others simply live in their rickshaws or on the street. They work for more than 12 hours at a time, earning about 100 rupees ($2.50 USD) a day. Their top priority is paying the rent on their vehicles, and then buying food and shelter. Any extra money goes to their families.

For the last ten years, the government has been trying to get rid of rickshaws. City authorities say they want to modernize Kolkata's image. They also want to reduce traffic congestion. "We must be fair to the cars and buses that are **crawling** because of the rickshaws," one city official said.

What does the future hold for rickshaw pullers? Most are 40 to 60 years old and have no other job skills. Local authorities have talked about programs to retrain the pullers. They could drive auto-rickshaws, for example, work in parking lots, or make traditional crafts. However, nothing has been done to start these programs, and rickshaw pullers are understandably very worried about the future. "I'll try anything, even learning a new job, if it will help my family," one puller said.

Mass Transit System,
Bangkok, Thailand

go to school
go shopping
go to work
visit your friends
go to another city

## Communication

**A** Tell your partner about the form of transportation you or your family members use for the activities in the box.

**B** With your partner, make a chart and list some of the positive and negative aspects of the forms of transportation you mentioned in exercise **A.**

| Form of transportation | Positive aspects | Negative aspects |
| --- | --- | --- |
| | | |
| | | |

## Writing

*Dear Editor,*

*Sincerely,*

**A** How would you improve the transportation system in your city? Write a letter to the editor of a newspaper explaining your ideas. Begin your letter "Dear Editor,". End it with "Sincerely," and sign your name.

**B** Exchange letters with your partner. Ask each other questions about your ideas, and make suggestions for changes and improvements.

**C** Revise your letter based on your partner's suggestions.

**D** 🔅 **GOAL CHECK** ✔ **Make recommendations for improving transportation**

Read your letter aloud to the class, and answer any questions your classmates have about your ideas.

Bicycle messenger in
New York City

## Before You Watch

**A** 🔁 Discuss the question with a partner: How many kinds of transportation
can people use to get around your city? Rank them from fastest
to slowest in your notebook.

## While You Watch

**A** ▶️ Watch the video and complete the summary.

Every day, in the city of (1) _____ , thousands of documents and

packages are delivered by people riding (2) _____ . Their work

is dangerous because they must ride very (3) _____ in heavy traffic.

Even though it's difficult, most messengers (4) _____ their work.

**B** ▶️ Watch the video again and write in your notebook one reason why . . .

1. bicycle messengers like their job:
2. police officers get angry at messengers:
3. people in New York dislike bicycle messengers:
4. bicycle messengers don't like people in cars:

## After You Watch / Communication

**A** 🎭 What could be done to make bicycle messengers' jobs safer? With your
group, list as many ideas as you can. Then choose a role from the box and
role-play a meeting with the city council. Make three recommendations to
the city council about rules bicycle messengers should follow.

a bicycle messenger
a police officer
a parent with small children
a business owner

# Competition

Competitor in bull race in West Sumatra,
Indonesia

**Look at the photo, answer the questions:**

**1** What type of competition is this?

**2** Besides sports, what other situations can you think of that involve competition?

**UNIT 8 GOALS**

1. Talk about sports

2. Explain which sport is best for you

3. Talk about positive and negative aspects of competition

4. Discuss competitive advantages

## Vocabulary

**A** Read the article. Notice the words in blue.

Competitive sports can be a lot of fun, especially when you or your team wins a game or a match. On the other hand, some athletes show poor sportsmanship when they lose—getting angry or even worse. In order to understand this kind of bad behavior, it's important to remember the amount of daily training that athletes do and whether they play an individual sport, such as golf, or a team sport, such as soccer. For them, they don't just lose a game; they lose the time and effort they invested before the game ever began.

**Word Focus**

We rarely use the word *sportsmanship* by itself. We talk about *good sportsmanship* or *poor sportsmanship*.

**B** Write each word in blue next to its synonym or definition.

1. _____ practicing
2. _____ group of players
3. _____ one person
4. _____ players
5. _____ behavior in sports
6. _____ does better than everyone else
7. _____ having winners and losers
8. _____ not do as well as everyone else
9. _____ sports event in basketball, etc.
10. _____ sports event in tennis, etc.

## Grammar: Negative questions

| | |
|---|---|
| Negative questions in the simple present begin with *don't/doesn't* or *aren't/isn't*. | **Don't** you want to go downtown with us? (The speaker may expect you to say *yes*.) |
| Use negative questions to show that we expect a certain answer or to show attitudes such as surprise. | **Aren't** you happy about winning? (The speaker may be surprised because you don't look happy.) |
| Negative questions can also begin with the negative form of a modal such as *won't, can't, shouldn't,* or *wouldn't*. | **Shouldn't** you call your parents? **Won't** they be worried? |
| Answer negative questions in the same way as regular questions. | **Didn't** the Tigers win yesterday? **Yes, they did.** (if they won) **No, they didn't.** (if they didn't win) |

**A** Read each situation and circle the correct answer.

Word Focus

The sporting event called a **soccer game** in the U.S. is called a **football match** in the U.K.

1. Your friend offers you an orange.
   **You:** No, thank you.
   **Your friend:** Oh, don't you like oranges?
   Your friend is probably ( surprised | angry ).

2. A student gives an assignment to his teacher.
   **Teacher:** Wasn't this due yesterday?
   **Student:** Yes, it was. I'm sorry it's late.
   The teacher is probably ( happy | annoyed ).

3. You and a friend are talking about last week's soccer game.
   **You:** Now the team might not be in the World Cup.
   **Your friend:** But didn't they win last week's game?
   Your friend thinks the team ( did | did not ) win last week's game.

4. You arrive home after a long bus trip and you look tired.
   **Your mother:** Aren't you glad to be home?
   Your mother expects you to say ( yes | no ).

**B** 🗩 Work with a partner. Think of a possible situation for each of these negative questions. Imagine and practice the conversations.

- Don't you have any money?
- Doesn't the game start at two thirty?
- Isn't your sister a swimmer?
- Aren't you cold?
- Aren't these your glasses?
- Don't you need this?

## Conversation

**A** 🔊 6 Listen to the conversation with your book closed. What do Milena and Betty plan to do tonight?

**Milena:** How about the tennis match last night. Sanders acted crazy!
**Betty:** Really? What did he do?
**Milena:** Didn't you see it? He got really angry and broke his tennis racket.
**Betty:** No, I didn't, but I'm surprised. Sanders is usually such a good sportsman.
**Milena:** I know, but not last night! Well, I should get going.
**Betty:** Aren't you going to join us for dinner?
**Milena:** No, not tonight. The finals start at seven o'clock.
**Betty:** You're a true tennis fan. Well, have fun watching!

**B** 🗩 Practice the conversation with a partner. Switch roles and practice it again.

**C** 🗩 **GOAL CHECK** ✔ **Talk about sports**

Have a new conversation about sports. Use negative questions if you expect your partner to say *yes* or to show surprise.

*Tae kwon do* is a popular
martial art.

| baseball | soccer |
| badminton | tennis |
| skiing | martial arts |
| swimming | bicycling |
| volleyball | boxing |
| basketball | golf |

## Listening

**A** 🔗 Work with a partner. Write each sport in the correct place in the diagram.

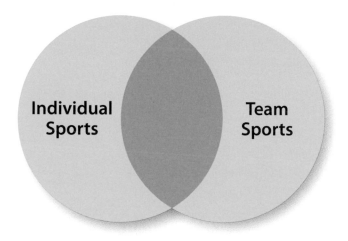

_____ golf
_____ volleyball
_____ a marathon
_____ the soccer team
_____ martial arts
_____ basketball

**B** 🔗 Discuss these questions with a partner. Give reasons for your answers. What type of person enjoys playing individual sports? What type of person enjoys playing team sports?

**C** 🔊 7 Listen to three people talking. Decide which sport in the box would be best for each person.

1.  Rita should probably play:

2.  Chris should probably train for:

3.  Susan should probably sign up for:

**Real Language**

When you *count on someone*, you depend on them to do something that's important to you.

**D** 🔗 🔊 7 How did you make your choices in exercise **C**? Listen again and take brief notes on what the speakers say in your notebook. Then share your reasons.

## Pronunciation: Intonation to show surprise

**A** 🔊 8 We can use rising intonation in statements to show that we're surprised by something we just heard. The rising intonation makes the statements sound like questions. Listen and repeat these sentences.

1. He left this morning?
2. You're joining a volleyball team?
3. They won by fifteen points?
4. He plays professional golf?

**B** 🔁 Practice the conversation with a partner. Use rising intonation to show surprise in the underlined sentences.

**Barb:** Is that your son, Arturo?
**Arturo:** Yes, that's Michael. It seems like he's always getting hurt.
**Barb:** <u>Aren't you worried</u>? He's not getting up.
**Arturo:** Oh, he'll be OK. There's the team doctor now.
**Barb:** I hope you're right. This is why I don't let my daughter play sports.
**Arturo:** <u>You don't let her</u>? But most kids love to play sports!
**Barb:** Sure, but they can also get hurt when they play.
**Arturo:** I think that's part of life.
**Barb:** I guess you're right. <u>Hey, isn't that Michael on the field</u>?
**Arturo:** That's him. He's up and running again!

## Communication

**A** 🔁 Take turns. Ask a partner these questions about personality types.

1. Are you an introvert (quiet, shy) or extrovert (social)?

2. Are you a perfectionist, or do you need outside pressure to motivate you?

3. Are you very focused when you do something (you forget about everything else), or are you aware of everything going on around you?

4. Do you like vigorous exercise, such as running, or more gentle exercise?

5. Do you like to concentrate on one thing for a long time, or do you prefer shorter activities that are constantly changing?

**B** 🔁 Recommend a sport for your partner to play based on his or her answers.

**C** 👥 **GOAL CHECK** ✔ **Explain which sport is best for you**

Tell the class which sport your partner recommended for you. Explain why the sport is a good match for your personality, or choose a different sport if you think it's not a good match.

## Language Expansion: Sports

**A** Write each word from the illustration below next to its correct meaning.

1. a large sign that shows the score at a sports event _____
2. someone who trains a person or a sports team _____
3. a prize given to the winner of a competition _____
4. the total number of points received in a sports event _____
5. the numbers that are added together to give the score _____
6. a metal disk given as a prize in a sports event _____

**B** Take turns. Ask and answer these questions about the illustration.

1. What was the final score of the championship game?
2. How many points did the winning team have?
3. What is the coach presenting to the team?
4. What is every player wearing around his neck?

## Grammar: Adjective clauses with object pronouns

| | |
|---|---|
| An adjective clause can modify a noun that is the object of a verb or a preposition. | He won <u>a medal</u>. It was made of gold.<br>The medal **that he won** was made of gold. |
| Use the object pronoun *that* or *which* in adjective clauses about things. | I'm on <u>a team</u>. It was formed last year.<br>The team **which I'm on** was formed last year. |
| Use the object pronoun *that* or *who* (or *whom* in writing or formal speaking) in adjective clauses about people. | We met <u>a woman</u>. She plays basketball.<br>The woman **that/who(m) we met** plays basketball. |

**A** Complete the journal entry with *that*, *which*, or *whom*.

> Yesterday, I ran into an old friend (1) _____ I hadn't seen in several months. We started chatting, and I told my friend about the new job (2) _____ I got last week. As I talked to her, I could see something that surprised me. It was envy! Most of the people (3) _____ I had told about my job were happy for me, but this friend has always been very competitive.
>
> The lesson (4) _____ I learned that day was simple: It's possible to be too competitive. Competitiveness is not helpful in every situation. Instead, just forget about the envy and be happy for the friends (5) _____ you care about.

**B** Complete each sentence with your own ideas.

1. The kind of person who I like is _____ .
2. The sports that I prefer are _____ .
3. One activity that I dislike is _____ .
4. A person whom I met recently was _____ .

## Conversation

**A** 🔊 9 Listen to the conversation with your book closed. What does Dean decide to do?

**Dean:** Hi, Kirsten. Can I talk to you about something?

**Kirsten:** Sure. What is it?

**Dean:** Some of my friends want me to try out for the wrestling team, but I just don't have a competitive personality.

**Kirsten:** Well, some people are more competitive than others.

**Dean:** Right, and sometimes I am competitive. I think about my classmates who get good grades, and it motivates me to work harder.

**Kirsten:** There you go.

**Dean:** On the other hand, I don't really like people that always want to be the best. Sometimes other people are the best.

**Kirsten:** And you want to be happy for those other people.

**Dean:** Exactly! Maybe I could talk to a few guys on the wrestling team and find out if it's the right sport for me.

**B** 🔁 Practice the conversation. Then talk about when you have competed for something.

**C** 🔁 **GOAL CHECK** ✔ **Talk about positive and negative aspects of competition**

Talk about times when being competitive is good motivation. Then talk about when being competitive brings out the worst in people.

**Engage!**

Are the lessons that competitive sports teach us helpful or harmful?

**Real Language**

You can say *there you go* when you agree with someone or you think someone has a good idea.

## Reading

**A** 🔁 Use a dictionary to look up the meanings of the words in blue.

You may think that in sports, winning is always about strength, speed, and other athletic abilities, but two anthropologists from England wanted to know whether the color of athletes' *clothing* can affect the final scores of sporting events!

The scientists already knew that animals respond to the color red. Having red on their bodies helps some animals to attract a mate, and dominant male animals sometimes have more red on their bodies than non-dominant males. Is it possible that human beings respond to red in a similar way?

**B** As you read the article, take notes on the scientific research.

- the names and university of the scientists who did the research in Athens

- what those scientists wanted to find out

- the method they used (How did they do their research?)

- the results of their research

**C** Read the statements. Circle **T** for *true*, **F** for *false*, or **NI** for *no information* (if the information is not in the reading).

1. Hill and Barton are both interested in primates.     **T F NI**

2. Female mandrills use red coloration to attract a mate.     **T F NI**

3. Red was not an advantage for zebra finches.     **T F NI**

4. The red plastic rings were left on the finches permanently.     **T F NI**

5. Hill and Barton believe athletes in red are more likely to win.     **T F NI**

6. Hill and Barton think some Olympic athletes cheated.     **T F NI**

Athens, Greece

IN SPORTS, RED IS THE **WINNING** COLOR

When **players** of a game are equally matched, the team dressed in red is more likely to win, according to a new study.

British anthropologists Russell Hill and Robert Barton of the University of Durham reached that conclusion by studying the **final scores** of boxing, *tae kwon do*, Greco-Roman wrestling, and freestyle wrestling matches at the 2004 Summer Olympics in Athens, Greece.

In each event, Olympic staff randomly assigned red or blue clothing or body protection to competitors. When competitors were equally matched with their opponents in fitness and skill, the athletes wearing red were more likely to win.

"Where there was a large point difference—presumably because one athlete was far **better than** the other—color had no effect on the outcome," Barton said. "Where there was a small point difference, the effect of color was sufficient to tip the balance."

Joanna Setchell, a primate researcher at the University of Cambridge in England, has found similar results in nature. Her work with the large African monkeys known as mandrills shows that red coloration gives males an advantage when it comes to mating. The finding that red also has an advantage in human sporting events does not surprise her, and she adds that "the idea of the study is very clever."

Hill and Barton got the idea for their study from a mutual interest in animals—"red seems to be the color, across species, that signals male dominance," Barton said. For example, studies by Setchell, the Cambridge primate researcher, show that **dominant** male mandrills have increased red coloration in their faces and rumps. In another study, scientists put red plastic rings on the legs of male zebra finches, which increased the birds' success in finding a **mate**.

Barton said he and Hill speculated that "there might be a similar effect in humans." Hill and Barton found their answer by viewing Olympic competitors in the ring, on the mat, and in the field. "Across a range of sports, we find that wearing red is consistently associated with a higher probability of winning," the researchers write.

Barton adds that this discovery of red's advantage might lead to new rules on sports uniforms. In the Olympic matches which he studied, for example, it is possible that some medal winners may have had an unintended advantage—their clothing!

**Coach speaks to the players during basketball Game**

sleep    training schedule
diet    advice from coaches
_____
_____
_____

## Communication

**A**  A competitive advantage is something that makes you more likely to win or succeed. Besides wearing the color red, what other things give an athlete a competitive advantage? Discuss the topics in the box with a partner and add some of your own ideas.

**B** Join another pair of students and share your ideas from exercise **A**.

## Writing

**A** In your notebook, make a bullet-point list of advice for a coach to give to athletes. Use phrases such as:

- It's a good idea to …
- It's absolutely necessary to …
- You should always …

- Be sure to …
- Don't forget to …

**B** Read your list to your group and explain how your advice would give an athlete a competitive advantage. Ask your classmates to comment on your ideas.

**C** **GOAL CHECK** ✓ Discuss competitive advantages

With your group, discuss what gives people a competitive advantage outside of sports; for example:

> I have a friend who manages his time well. That's certainly an advantage at school.

at school    in a career    in social situations    other _____

**Riders in action in Utah, USA**

In the huge, open lands of the American West, herding cattle is one way to make a living. The image of the cowboy on his horse is a familiar one, but in reality, women also participate in ranch work. This reality can be seen in the rodeo, where cowboys and cowgirls compete in roping young steer and riding adult bulls. Throwing a rope around a steer is something ranchers must do to mark the steers as their property. On the other hand, riding on the back of a large bull is purely for sport— a dangerous sport. But that danger doesn't stop the men and women who love the rodeo.

## Before You Watch

**A** Read about the origins of rodeo competitions. Use a dictionary to find out the meanings of the words in blue.

## While You Watch

**A** ▶ Watch the video and check (✓) each expression when you hear it.

____ **a man's sport** = a sport that was traditionally played by men

____ **to go head-to-head with someone** = to compete directly with someone

____ **to be in the saddle** = to ride on horseback; to use horses to do one's work

____ **times are changing** = traditional ways are being replaced with new ways

____ **it seems like an eternity** = it seems to take a very long time

## After You Watch / Communication

**A** 🔁 Discuss the quotation in the box with a partner. In your opinion, what does the quote tell us about Ms. Crawford?

**B** 👥 Rodeo competitions test the skills of ranchers. Choose a job. Then imagine a new sport that tests the skills people need to do that job. Think of two "events" people can compete in. What must they do to win the events?

A lot of times I like to show up, and the guys are like, "There ain't no way she's gonna ride." I like to go out there and do my best and show them I can ride because they think I can't. You've got to keep your head up and say, "I'm just as good as you all are."

DeDee Crawford, 2001 world champion female bull rider

# Danger

A firefighter drives through a forest fire in Seeley Lake, Montana.

OBJECTS IN MIRROR ARE CLOSER THAN THEY APPEAR

## UNIT 9 GOALS

1. Discuss ways to stay safe

2. Talk about dangerous work

3. Discuss personal emergencies

4. Discuss dangerous situations

## GOAL 1: Discuss Ways to Stay Safe

_____ mosquito
_____ shark
_____ elephant
_____ smoking
_____ alligator
_____ going to bed

▲ A great white shark

## Vocabulary

**A** 🔗 Look at the items in the box and rate them: 1 = very dangerous, 2 = somewhat dangerous, 3 = not dangerous.

**B** Read the information below. Which answers would you change in exercise **A**?

What's _really_ dangerous?
- Scientists estimate that mosquitoes kill 3 million people in the world every year.
- Over 125 deaths a year are caused by elephants (mostly in Africa and Asia).
- Spiders kill 6 people in the U.S. every year with their poison. The risk is higher for children.
- In the last 60 years, alligators have killed 18 people in Florida.
- Around 1,909 people have been killed by sharks since 1530—about 5 per year. Many people survive shark attacks.
- Tobacco plays a role in 18.1 percent of all deaths in the U.S. It has over 30 substances that are toxic.
- Every year, 36,000 people are injured in accidents with their beds. These accidents can be easily prevented.

**C** Write the words in blue next to their meanings.

1. chance that something bad will happen _____

2. something that kills people _____

3. hurt a person's body _____

4. to guess the amount or extent _____

5. containing poison _____

6. solids, liquids, or gases _____

7. stopped from happening _____

8. live through a dangerous situation _____

## Grammar: Tag questions

| Use tag questions to check information in a sentence that you're not sure about or to confirm your opinion. | That kind of snake is poisonous, **isn't it?** (I'm not sure.)<br>You started smoking again, **didn't you?** (I think you probably did.) |
| --- | --- |
| Affirmative sentences have negative tag questions, and negative sentences have affirmative tag questions. | You're a student, **aren't you?**<br>You're not allergic to bee stings, **are you?** |
| Answer tag questions in the same way as other questions. | I'm too late to help you, **aren't I?**<br>**Yes, you are.** (If he is too late.)<br>**No, you're not.** (If he's not too late.) |

**A** Match each sentence with the correct tag question.

1. Tigers don't hunt at night, _____
2. Accidents injure many people, _____
3. Ron didn't start smoking, _____
4. There's safety information on the label, _____
5. She's at risk for a heart attack, _____
6. We aren't in an earthquake zone, _____

a. did he?
b. isn't there?
c. are we?
d. don't they?
e. do they?
f. isn't she?

**B** Add tag questions to these sentences.

1. Some kinds of fish are poisonous, _____?
2. We don't have dangerous weather here, _____?
3. There isn't any danger in this classroom, _____?
4. There aren't any dangerous animals in cities, _____?
5. The exits are clearly marked in this building, _____?
6. They don't allow toxic substances in food, _____?

▲ A zebra lionfish

## Conversation

**A** 🔊 **10** Listen to the conversation. Why is Ruthie worried?

**Ruthie:** You know, I really don't like driving. It scares me to death.
**Dan:** Really? Why is that?
**Ruthie:** Well, it's dangerous, isn't it? Just think of all the people who are killed in their cars every year!
**Dan:** That's true, but there's a lot you can do to stay safe.
**Ruthie:** Like what?
**Dan:** For one thing, you should stop texting or talking on your cell phone when you drive. That causes a lot of accidents.
**Ruthie:** I suppose you're right.
**Dan:** And you should keep enough distance from other cars.
**Ruthie:** That's not a bad idea.

**B** 🔄 What can you do to stay safe in these situations? Think of several ideas with a partner. Then make new conversations.

> thunderstorms    flying on an airplane    fixing the roof

**C** 🔄 **GOAL CHECK** ✓ **Discuss ways to stay safe**

Talk to your partner about how to stay safe in another situation.

> **Engage!**
>
> In informal speaking, we say something *scares us to death* if it frightens us a lot. What scares you to death?

## Listening

**A** 🔊 **11** Listen to a radio program about an unusual job. Then read the statements and choose the correct answer.

1. The job of a food taster is to make sure that food is _____ .
   **a.** delicious   **b.** healthy   **c.** not poisoned

2. Today, there are _____ food tasters.
   **a.** no more   **b.** only a few   **c.** many

**B** 🔊 **11** Listen again. Then complete the summary of the radio program.

In the past, kings and queens used food tasters to protect themselves against (1) _____. Their job was to taste all the food in the king's meal and make sure it was (2) _____ to eat. Mathura Prasad was a food taster for the lord of Castle Mandawa in (3) _____. When the food was ready, some of it was fed to a (4) _____. Then Mathura Prasad (5) _____ it before it went to the lord's table. Food tasters have a long (6) _____. For example, Christopher Columbus used (7) _____ to test food on his trips. Today, most countries don't use food tasters, but in (8) _____, soldiers sometimes taste the president's food. And in (9) _____, the king's food is checked by mice.

▲ Mathura Prasad, food taster to the *thakur*, or lord, of Castle Mandawa

**C** 🔁 Discuss these questions with a partner. What were the good points and bad points of Mathura Prasad's job? Why do you think he did this job?

## Pronunciation: Intonation of tag questions

Rajasthan, India

**A** 🔊 **12** The intonation of tag questions shows how sure we are of the answer. If we are sure and want agreement, we use falling intonation. If we are not sure and want to check the information, we use rising intonation. Listen and repeat the sentences, noticing the intonation.

1. Mathura had a dangerous job, didn't he? (sure)

2. There aren't many food tasters now, are there? (not sure)

**B** 🔁 🔊 **13** Listen to the statements and circle *sure* or *not sure*. Then practice reading them to a partner.

1. That plant isn't poisonous, is it?            sure    not sure
2. He knows all about it, doesn't he?           sure    not sure
3. That bridge doesn't look safe, does it?       sure    not sure
4. You were here yesterday, weren't you?         sure    not sure
5. His name is David, isn't it?                  sure    not sure
6. This exercise was easy, wasn't it?            sure    not sure

## Communication

**A** Complete the chart with your ideas about dangerous jobs.

| Description | Bad things about the job | Good things about the job |
|---|---|---|
| firefighter: puts out fires in houses and other buildings | – could be burned – has to work really fast | – saves people's lives |
| race car driver: | | |
| tiger trainer: | | |

**B** 🔁 Role-play a newspaper reporter interviewing the people in exercise **A.** Use tag questions to check information and add your own ideas.

**C** 🔁 | **GOAL CHECK** ✔  **Talk about dangerous work**

Discuss these questions with a partner.

1. Would you like to do any of the jobs in exercise **A?** Why or why not?
2. What other jobs are dangerous? Why?
3. Why are people attracted to dangerous jobs?

> You run into burning buildings, don't you?

> That's right. It's incredibly hot in there!

# **GOAL 3:** Discuss Personal Emergencies

## Language Expansion: Expressions for emergencies

**A** What should you say? Write the correct sentence for each picture.

> Where's the nearest pharmacy?    Where's the emergency room?
> Where's the nearest hospital?    Call the police!
> Call the fire department!    Call an ambulance!

1. _____

2. _____

3. _____

4. _____

5. _____

6. _____

> **If your child swallows something toxic, you should ask, "Where's the nearest hospital?"**

**B** Think of one more situation for each of the sentences in exercise **A**.

## Grammar: Adverbial clauses of time

| | |
|---|---|
| Adverbial clauses give more information about the main verb of the sentence. | They ran out of the house **when** they saw the fire. |
| An adverbial clause of time answers the question: *When?* | The ambulance will come **as soon as** it can get here. |
| | Kim always looks around **before** she gets out of her car. |
| The adverbial clause can come before or after the main clause. | **After** Jack broke his arm, he was more careful. |
| If the adverbial clause comes before the main clause, it is followed by a comma. | **While** you're in the hospital waiting room, you can read magazines. |

**A** Underline the adverbial clause. Then rewrite the sentences in your notebook with the adverbial clause first.

1. I take a shower and eat breakfast before I go to class.

2. He called the fire department as soon as he saw the flames.

3. We feel nervous whenever we have a test.

4. I like to watch the news on TV while I eat breakfast.

5. I screamed when I saw the snake.

**B** What should you do in these situations? Complete the sentences with adverbial clauses of time.

1. When you see a car accident, you should _____ _____.

2. You should _____ _____ as soon as you smell smoke in a building.

3. Before you climb a ladder, you should _____ .

4. You should _____ after you are bitten by an animal.

5. You should _____ while you're waiting for an ambulance to arrive.

## Conversation

**A** 🔊 14  Listen to the phone conversation with your book closed. What was the problem at Jen's house?

**Jen:** Hello?

**Lily:** Hi, Jen. It's Lily, your neighbor ... Are you OK? I saw the fire truck in front of your house!

**Jen:** Don't worry, we're fine. We had a fire in our kitchen, but everything's OK now.

**Lily:** Oh, no! What happened?

**Jen:** I was cooking dinner, and I went to check on the baby. When I went back, the kitchen was full of black smoke!

**Lily:** How awful!

**Jen:** As soon as I saw the smoke, I called the fire department. After I called them, I took the baby out of the house.

**Lily:** Did it take them long to get there?

**Jen:** Only a few minutes. They put out the fire before it got very far. But my whole house smells like smoke now.

**Lily:** I'm so glad you're OK!

**Real Language**

We say *Oh no!* or *How awful!* when someone tells us about something very bad that happened.

**B** 🗘 Practice the conversation with a partner.

**C** 🗘 **GOAL CHECK** ✓ **Discuss personal emergencies**

Tell a partner about an emergency or serious problem that you had.

## GOAL 4: Discuss Dangerous Situations

### Reading

**A** 🔄 Which situations do you think are the most dangerous? Rank the items in the list below. Share your ideas with a partner.

_____ 1. driving or riding in a car

_____ 2. exploring a cave

_____ 3. flying in an airplane

_____ 4. walking at night in a city you don't know

_____ 5. working in a mine

**B** 🔄 Read the text. Circle the correct option. Compare your answers with a partner.

1. U.S. Airways Flight 1549 crashed ( on land | in water ).

2. Ric Elias is a ( pilot | businessman ).

3. Elias learned ( one | three ) important lessons because of the crash.

4. He understood he wanted to be a better ( parent | leader ).

5. In 2012, Elias helped start a ( university | scholarship ) for immigrants to the U.S.

**C** Write *True* or *False* next to the statements below.

_____ 1. Many people were killed when Flight 1549 crashed.

_____ 2. Elias decided to spend more time with people he loves.

_____ 3. Elias believes that it is more important to be right than happy.

_____ 4. Ric Elias wants to help other people succeed.

_____ 5. Elias believes he was lucky to survive the plane crash.

**TED** Ideas worth spreading

**Ric Elias** Entrepreneur, CEO of Red Ventures

# THREE THINGS I LEARNED WHILE MY PLANE CRASHED

On January 15, 2009, US Airways flight 1549 crash-landed on the Hudson River in New York City. A flock of large geese had flown into its engines and caused both of them to fail. Due to a combination of pilot skill and pure luck, everyone on the plane survived the accident. And it's safe to guess that most, if not all of them, changed the way they think about their lives as a result.

Although it is an experience that he hopes no one else has to have, passenger Ric Elias learned a lot that day. He says that three important lessons came out of that terrifying moment. The first is that in a life-or-death situation, "everything changes in an instant." He realized that it was important to do the things he wanted to do without postponing them. Whether it is fixing a friendship that has problems or going on an adventurous vacation, Elias says we shouldn't wait.

As the plane went down, the second lesson Elias learned was that it was important to eliminate negative energy from his life. He saw that he had spent too much time on winning arguments and feeling important. Now, he says, "I no longer try to be right; I choose to be happy."

The final important lesson Elias learned was that although it wasn't frightening to look death in the eye, it was sad. He realized the only thing he wanted was to see his children grow up. He understood that "the only thing that matters in my life is being a great dad." He encourages other parents to be the best mothers and fathers they can be, above all else.

Since then, Elias has lived those lessons. Even though he is the CEO of a growing company, he has also taken time to do good works. In 2012, he contributed $1 million toward the founding of Golden

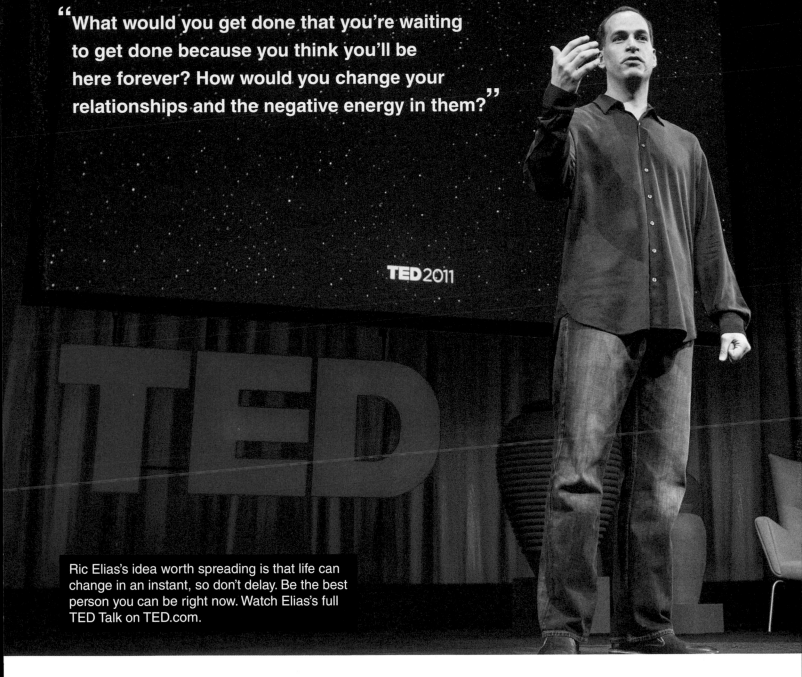

"What would you get done that you're waiting to get done because you think you'll be here forever? How would you change your relationships and the negative energy in them?"

TED2011

Ric Elias's idea worth spreading is that life can change in an instant, so don't delay. Be the best person you can be right now. Watch Elias's full TED Talk on TED.com.

Door Scholars, which provides scholarships for immigrant students who want to attend university. Elias says he has also improved his relationships with his wife, family, and friends.

As Elias remembers that cold winter's day in 2009, he knows "I was given the gift of a miracle, of not dying that day. I was given another gift, which was to be able to see into the future and come back and live differently." If you could look into your own future, what would you change now?

*crash-land* to land (an airplane, helicopter, etc.) in an unusual way because of an emergency
*flock* a group of birds or animals
*postpone* to decide that something which had been planned for a particular time will be done at a later time instead
*eliminate* to remove (something that is not wanted or needed)
*miracle* a very amazing or unusual event, thing, or achievement

Planning for dangerous situations is important. Everyone should have an emergency plan (1) _____ they are actually in a dangerous situation. For example, (2) _____ you stay in a hotel, look for the emergency exits. (3) _____ you are aware of danger, put your plan into action. (4) _____ you are safely outside, call the police or fire department. Remember, it's too late to plan for an emergency (5) _____ you are in the middle of one!

## Writing

**A** Add tag questions to the sentences.

1. Rick Elias learned important lessons, _____?

2. It's a miracle that no one was injured in the crash, _____?

3. We should all think about what needs to change in our lives, _____?

4. Everything changes in a life-or-death situation, _____?

5. Everyone can take time to do good things for others, _____?

**B** Complete the article in the margin about preparing for emergencies, using the adverbial expressions below. Then write a paragraph about emergency preparation.

after   as soon as   before   when   whenever

## Communication

**A** 🔁 Think about dangerous situations people face. How could they be made safer? Share your ideas with a partner.

**B** 🔁 **GOAL CHECK** ✓ **Discuss dangerous situations**

Share your ideas about dangerous situations. Can we prepare for every possible danger in life? Is it possible to be *too* careful? Give reasons for your opinions.

▲ iron

## Before You Watch

**A** 🔁 Work with a partner and discuss the questions.

1. Are the appliances in the photos dangerous?
2. How could they be dangerous?

## While You Watch

**A** ▶ Watch the video. Circle **T** for *true* and **F** for *false*.

1. Underwriters Laboratories (UL) was started in 1994.  **T   F**
2. Some of the tests at UL are the same as in the past.  **T   F**
3. The *drop test* is a test for appliances.  **T   F**
4. Engineers at UL only test the correct way to use an appliance.  **T   F**
5. At the end of the day, UL employees can keep the appliances.  **T   F**
6. Employees sometimes call UL *the Fun House*.  **T   F**

▲ toaster

▲ microwave

## After You Watch / Communication

**A** 🔁 If a person uses a product incorrectly and gets hurt, who is responsible—the person or the maker of the product? Explain your reasons to a partner.

**B** 👥 Imagine you are a group of safety engineers, like the ones in the video. Choose a common appliance. Make a list of ways that people might use this appliance incorrectly, and plan the tests that you will do. Share your ideas with the class. (DON'T do any real tests!)

▲ blender

# **TED**TALKS

## A LIFE LESSON FROM A VOLUNTEER FIREFIGHTER

## Before You Watch

are burning through the walls of a building, volunteer firefighters ignore the heavy (4) _____ on their backs and run in to save the (5) _____, their family, and even their pets.

**A** 🔄 Look at the picture and answer the questions with a partner.

**1.** Where is this person?

**2.** What is he doing?

**3.** How do you think he is feeling?

**B** Like the man in the picture, Mark Bezos is a firefighter. He described this dangerous and exciting work in a talk at TED. Here are some words you will hear in his TED Talk. Complete the paragraph with the correct words. Not all words will be used.

> **flames** *n.* the hot, glowing gas that can be seen when a fire is burning
> **footrace** *n.* a running race
> **homeowner** *n.* a person who owns a home, or an apartment
> **load** *n.* the amount of goods or material that is carried
> **remarkable** *adj.* unusual or surprising
> **vocation** *n.* a strong desire to spend your life doing a certain kind of work

Volunteer firefighters are (1) _____ people. Although they have other jobs, they also feel a strong (2) _____ to help others. Even when (3) _____

**C** Look at the pictures on the next page. Check (✓) the information that you predict you will hear in the TED Talk.

_____ **1.** There are many volunteer firefighters around the world.

_____ **2.** Being a volunteer firefighter is very important to me.

_____ **3.** My colleague was assigned to rescue the homeowner's dog.

## While You Watch

**A** ▶ Watch the TED Talk. Circle the main idea.

**1.** If you are interested in volunteering, there are many ways to help in your community.

**2.** Sometimes the small things we do for others are more important than we think they are.

**3.** Even though it can be dangerous, it is very rewarding to be a volunteer firefighter.

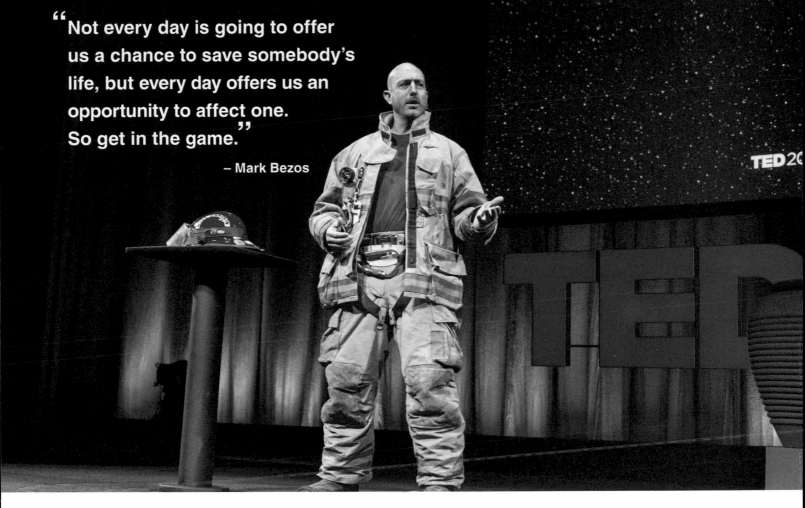

> **"Not every day is going to offer us a chance to save somebody's life, but every day offers us an opportunity to affect one. So get in the game."**
>
> – Mark Bezos

TED 20

**B** ▶ The photos below relate to the ideas in the TED Talk. Watch the talk again, and write the letter of the caption under the correct photo.

**a.** Mark Bezos is proud of his work as a volunteer firefighter.

**b.** We can all make a difference in someone's life.

**c.** Volunteers can also help clean up parks.

**d.** Bezos felt a bit jealous of his colleague who rescued a dog.

**1.** ___

**2.** ___

**3.** ___

**4.** ___

**Challenge!** 🔁 What do you think Mark Bezos enjoys the most about his work as a volunteer firefighter? Share your ideas with a partner.

# **TED**TALKS

## A LIFE LESSON FROM A VOLUNTEER FIREFIGHTER

## After You Watch

**A** Complete the summary with the words in the box.

| committed | exciting |
|---|---|
| homeowner | volunteer |
| professional | difference |

Mark Bezos is not a (1) _____ firefighter, but he's very

(2) _____ to the fire company he works with. As a

(3) _____, he receives assignments from the fire captain.

Sometimes, he gets an (4) _____ assignment, but other

times they don't seem that way. At his first fire, the captain asked Bezos

to get the (5) _____ shoes from a burning house. Even

though it seemed like a small thing, Bezos later learned that it made a big

(6) _____ to her. He learned that day that it's important to take

every opportunity to help others, no matter how small it may seem.

**B** Match the phrases to complete sentences from the TED Talk.

**Cause**

1. ____ Mark Bezos is the
2. ____ Bezos believes we should all
3. ____ One way we can help others is to
4. ____ We can also help by
5. ____ It's not hard to make a

**Effect**

a. cleaning up our local park.
b. serve food at a soup kitchen.
c. Head of Development for a non-profit company that helps poor people.
d. difference in our community.
e. look for ways to help others.

**C** Read the statements below. Circle the ones that paraphrase Mark Bezos' ideas.

1. Everyone should try to volunteer as a firefighter.

2. You don't always get to do what you want to do.

3. If you can help another person, don't wait.

4. We can find ways to contribute to society every day.

Young volunteers
cleaning up a beach

## Project

Mark Bezos encourages us to take every opportunity we can to help others. He believes that even a small act of kindness can make someone's life better. Use his ideas to survey your classmates about volunteering in your community.

**A** Look at the list of ways to volunteer. Circle the ones that are possible to do in your community.

| | |
|---|---|
| visiting sick or elderly people | cleaning up a park |
| collecting used clothes | feeding people at a soup kitchen |
| helping young children | helping at an animal shelter |

**B** 🔁 Compare your choices in exercise **A** with a partner. Are there any volunteer opportunities you'd like to add to the list?

**C** 🔆 Survey your classmates. Write a question for each item in your notebook. Ask a follow-up question for details. Answer your classmates' questions.

| | Question | Name | Details |
|---|---|---|---|
| **1.** way to help the sick and elderly | | | |
| **2.** way to help in education | | | |
| **3.** way to help the environment | | | |
| **4.** way to help animals | | | |

**Challenge!** In addition to being a volunteer firefighter, Mark Bezos has a full-time job in New York City. Go to TED.com and read more about Bezos in his speaker profile. What can you learn about his life? How are his full-time job and his role as a volunteer firefighter connected?

> **Pedro, what's a way you could help sick and elderly people?**

> **I could read to them.**

> **Why does it interest you?**

### Presentation Strategy

**Storytelling**

Mark Bezos uses a humorous personal story to keep his audience engaged and to illustrate his larger message about the importance of helping others.

# Mysteries

Moai at Ahu Akivi beneath the milky way,
Easter Island, Chile

**Look at the photo, answer the questions:**

**1** What do you think of when you hear the word *mysteries*?

**2** What kinds of unsolved mysteries have you heard about?

## UNIT 10 GOALS

1. Speculate about mysteries

2. Discuss types of mysteries

3. Talk about plans you used to have

4. Explain a mysterious image

▲ Monument to ancestors on Easter Island, Chile

## Vocabulary

**A** Read the information. Notice the words in blue.

> Chile's Easter Island was first seen by an outsider, Dutch explorer Jacob Roggeveen, in 1722. Since that time, people have been trying to figure out the mysteries of the large stone statues called Moai. Even today, we wonder how people with no modern technology managed to carve the stone, and we speculate about how they moved the massive statues.
>
> The Moai were made between 900 and 1500 CE, so they're not prehistoric, but the native people of Easter Island have no written history of how the statues were made or of their purpose. Scientific investigations have revealed that the island was once covered in trees and palms, which could have been used to make ropes for moving the statues. The remains of dolphins in early garbage dumps are further evidence for the presence of trees, which must have been used for making canoes to carry fishermen out to sea. Much about Easter Island, however, is still a mystery.

**Word Focus**

Two verb + preposition combinations you should know are **search for,** and **speculate about.**

**B** Write each word in blue next to the correct meaning.

1. ___speculate___ make guesses about something
2. _____ research projects, studies
3. _____ clues or signs that something is true
4. _____ parts of something that are left after most of it is gone
5. _____ try to find out what happened or what is true
6. _____ showed something; made people aware of something
7. _____ shape stone, wood, or other hard materials using sharp objects
8. _____ very large and heavy
9. _____ describes people or things that existed before information was written down

## Grammar: Modals for speculating about the past

| Explanation | Example |
|---|---|
| Use the modals *may*, *might*, and *could* to speculate, or make guesses, about the past.<br>After the modal, use *have* + the past participle of a verb. | The people of Easter Island **may have rolled** the statues over logs.<br>They **might have used** fish oil to make the statues easier to move.<br>The Moai **could have represented** kings. |
| When we are almost certain about our speculation or guess, we use *must*. | They **must have had** a way to travel on the ocean. |

**A** Complete the sentences with the correct form of the verb and an appropriate modal.

1. We don't know what happened to Amelia Earhart, but we think her plane _____ (crash) on an island in the Pacific.

2. I don't know where my keys are, but I _____ (have) them with me when I left the apartment, because the door is locked.

3. We don't think it was really a UFO. It _____ (be) an unusual cloud or a large balloon.

4. The explorers _____ (run out) of food and water, or they _____ (get lost) in the mountains.

5. No one knows what happened to the treasure ship, but some people think it _____ (sink) in the Mediterranean Sea.

**B** Read the information in the box above. In your notebook, write five sentences with modals to speculate about Atlantis.

## Communication

**A** 🗘 Talk about these famous places. Use modals for speculating about the past.

1. The pyramids at Giza, Egypt, are the subject of much speculation. The largest of the three pyramids was completed some 4,500 years ago and was made from over 2 million massive stone blocks. How do you think workers constructed these pyramids?

2. The Nazca lines in Peru are a group of enormous pictures made by removing reddish surface stones to expose the light-colored ground below. Because of their large size, it's impossible to see any one of the pictures from the ground, and there are no nearby mountains. What do you think was the purpose of these pictures?

3. Archaeologists have discovered hundreds of stone spheres in Costa Rica. The largest of the nearly perfect spheres are more than two meters across! They were probably made between 200 BCE and 1500 CE, but no one knows how people were able to carve these perfectly geometric balls from solid stone.

**B** 🗘 | **GOAL CHECK** ✓ **Speculate about mysteries**

Talk to a partner about mysterious places or events in your country or your region of the world. Why are the places mysterious? What do you speculate about these places?

More than two thousand years ago, the philosopher Plato wrote about the lost island of Atlantis. It may have been a legend or simply fiction, but Plato wrote that Atlantis was an advanced and powerful nation that sank into the ocean in one unfortunate day and night.

> **The workers might have put the stones in boats on the Nile River.**

Illustration of a sea monster

## Listening

**A** 🔁 Discuss these questions with a partner.

1. Do you know any stories about sea monsters?

2. Do you think sea monsters might really exist?

3. Do you know what *fossils* are?

**B** 🔊 **15** Listen to an expert talking about sea monsters. Write the name of a place and the monster in your notebook.

**C** 🔊 **15** Listen again and choose the correct answer to each question.

1. According to the expert, at one time, sea monsters _____.
   **a.** didn't exist      **b.** might have existed      **c.** did exist

2. When scientists found fossils near Loch Ness, people speculated that Nessie might be _____.
   **a.** a skeleton      **b.** a dinosaur      **c.** a rock

3. According to legends, the Unktehila were destroyed by _____.
   **a.** snakes      **b.** Native Americans      **c.** Thunder Beings

4. Millions of years ago, _____ lived in North America.
   **a.** alligators      **b.** mosasaurs      **c.** crocodiles

5. Some Chinese dragons represented good luck because they could _____.
   **a.** bring rain      **b.** find fossils      **c.** sail in boats

### Engage!

Why do people enjoy mysteries?

**D** 🔁 🔊 **15** Listen again. Then discuss the questions with a partner.

1. Which sea monster story was the most interesting to you?

2. If you could talk to the expert, what questions would you ask?

## Pronunciation: Intonation: Finished and unfinished ideas

**A** 🔊 16  In a conversation, it's important to know when someone has finished speaking. One way speakers show that they are finished is falling intonation. When they are not finished, they may use steady or rising intonation. Listen to the finished and unfinished ideas in the box.

**B** 🔊 17  When you hear an unfinished idea, the speaker may plan to continue. Listen to the examples.

**C** 🔄  Practice these sentences with a partner. End the sentence with steady or rising intonation when you see three dots ( . . . ). End with falling intonation when you see a period ( . ).

1.  Loch Ness is 37 kilometers long and very deep.

2.  The pilot said he saw a large object flying beside the airplane.

3.  The ship's captain tried to send a radio message, . . .

4.  People see different things when they look at the painting.

5.  Some people may have dreams about the future, . . .

**D** 🔄  For each unfinished idea in exercise **C,** speculate about what the speaker will say next.

| Finished |
| --- |
| He thought he saw something in the water. |
| These stories can't possibly be true. |
| **Unfinished** |
| At first he thought it was a fish, . . . |
| But some people believe them, . . . |

## Conversation

**A** 🔊 18  Listen to the conversation with your book closed. Why does Tommy think Joan won't like the book?

| | |
| --- | --- |
| **Joan:** | Hi, Tommy. What are you reading? |
| **Tommy:** | It's a mystery novel—*The Clock Strikes at Midnight*. |
| **Joan:** | Is it any good? |
| **Tommy:** | It's all right, . . . |
| **Joan:** | Then maybe I'll read it when you're done. |
| **Tommy:** | Maybe not. I was going to say it's good, but I don't think you'd like it. |
| **Joan:** | Why not? I like mystery novels. |
| **Tommy:** | I know, but in this one, a young child is missing. I know you don't like to read about kidnappings, or murder, or . . . |
| **Joan:** | You're right. It doesn't sound like my kind of book. |

**B** 🔄  Practice the conversation with a partner. Then switch roles and practice it again.

**C** 🔄 | **GOAL CHECK** ✓ **Discuss types of mysteries**

Some people like a good ghost story. Others enjoy murder mysteries. Tell a partner about the kinds of mysteries you enjoy hearing about or reading about. Then talk about mysterious things that you'd rather not hear or read about.

**C**   **GOAL 3:** Talk About Plans You Used to Have

**Stonehenge, a prehistoric monument in Wiltshire, England**

## Language Expansion: Reacting to surprises

**A** 🔊 **19**   Listen to a tour guide talk about Stonehenge. Fill in the blanks as you listen.

**Tour guide:** You can see that Stonehenge is very old. In fact, people started building Stonehenge nearly _____ years ago.

**Tourist:** Wow!

**Tour guide:** That's right. And while no one really knows why Stonehenge was built, there are some things we do know. The largest stones you see are these *trilithons*—two huge upright stones with a third stone laid on top. On average, these stones are _____ meters high.

**Tourist:** That's amazing!

**Tour guide:** I agree. What's even more amazing is that prehistoric people transported these stones _____ kilometers. And that was without any modern machinery.

**Tourist:** Really?!

**Tour guide:** And would you believe that these smaller bluestones came from a site in Wales, around _____ kilometers away!

**Tourist:** You're kidding!

**Tour guide:** I'm not! And the builders of Stonehenge must have known a lot about transportation because each of these "smaller" stones weighs around _____ kilos!

**Tourist:** Remarkable!

**B** 🔊 **19**   Listen again and notice the way the tourists express their surprise.

**C** 👥   Talk about mysterious things you know about. Your classmates will use expressions from exercise **A** to show surprise.

## Grammar: The future in the past

| | |
|---|---|
| Use subject + *was/were* + *going to* + verb to talk about future plans that were made at a past time. | He **was going** to visit Stonehenge as soon as he could. |
| This structure sometimes means that the plans did not actually happen. | We **were going to** take the train from London, but we drove there instead. |

**A** Fill in the blanks to complete the future-in-the-past structure.

In 1501, the Portuguese explorer Gaspar Corte-Real left Portugal with three ships. He (1)_____ search for a route to India. He sailed northwest, and although he didn't reach India, he did find a land he called Terra Verde, or Greenland. Then, all three ships sailed south. They (2)_____ return to Portugal. Unfortunately, only two ships arrived in Lisbon. Corte-Real's ship was never seen again.

Then in 1502, Gaspar's brother Miguel Corte-Real set out on an expedition with two ships. He (3)_____ look for his brother. Unfortunately, no one knows whether he found Gaspar. After sailing for some time, Miguel had the two ships go separate ways, thinking they (4)_____ cover more area and have a better chance of locating Gaspar. But Miguel's ship never returned to Portugal.

That left one surviving brother, Vasco Annes, who asked the king for permission to launch a third expedition. He (5)_____ do what Miguel had failed to do—find his brother. Perhaps wisely, King Manuel refused to give Vasco Annes permission for the journey.

## Conversation

**A** 🔊 20 Listen to the conversation with your book closed. Why didn't Eric visit Takeda Castle?

**Lenora:** Hi! I was hoping I would see you! I want to hear all about your trip.

**Eric:** We had a wonderful time, except for one day.

**Lenora:** What happened?

**Eric:** We were going to visit Takeda Castle. They call it Japan's Machu Picchu.

**Lenora:** That sounds interesting.

**Eric:** Yes, it's in the mountains, and the view from there is supposed to be amazing.

**Lenora:** Is it very far from Kyoto?

**Eric:** Only about three hours. We were going to take the train, but that morning, my wife hurt her ankle.

**Lenora:** And, of course, you wanted to walk around the ruins.

**Eric:** Of course, and we wanted to hike from the train station to the castle, too.

**Lenora:** That's a shame, but now you have a good reason to go back to Japan.

▲ Takeda Castle in Hyogo, Japan

**B** 🔁 Practice the conversation with a partner. Then have new conversations about places you would like to visit.

**C** 🔁 **GOAL CHECK** ✔ **Talk about plans you used to have**

Tell a partner about plans you had for the future when you were a child. What were you going to be when you grew up? Where were you going to live? What was your life going to be like?

## Reading

**A** 🗪 Discuss these questions with a partner.

1. When you imagine scientists at work, where do you see them?

2. Do you think it's important to learn about prehistoric people?

**B** Try to figure out the meaning of each word in bold without using a dictionary.

1. trek _____

2. facing _____

3. handprints _____

4. shamanistic _____

5. fragile _____

**C** What do you think the scientists wondered when they first saw the Kalimantan cave paintings? Write three questions they might have asked themselves.

1. _____

2. _____

3. _____

**D** 🗪 Compare your questions with a partner's questions. Then speculate about the possible answers.

▲ Visitors looking at cave paintings

Indonesian Borneo

# HANDS ACROSS TIME

**Marang Mountains, Indonesia**

**T**hey're known as *cavers*—people whose idea of a good time is exploring dark and sometimes dangerous caves. And that was exactly what first drew Luc-Henri Fage to the Island of Borneo in 1988. His goal at the time was an adventurous **trek** across the island along with other cavers.

On that first trip to Borneo, Luc-Henri saw ancient charcoal drawings on the ceiling of a large rock overhang. When he returned to France, he couldn't find any information about rock art in the region, so he returned to Borneo. Over the years, he kept returning and was joined by a French archaeologist and an Indonesian anthropologist. They found numerous caves with not only drawings, but also mysterious and obviously very old paintings. Then, in 1999, they saw the hands for the first time.

Exploring the region of Kalimantan, the Indonesian part of Borneo, is not an easy task. There are no roads to the Marang Mountains, so Fage and the others made their way up the Bungulun River in canoes, camping along the way, at times **facing** storms and fire ants that tried to join the campers to get out of the rain. The Marang Mountains rise out of the hot, humid jungle below, and their steep sides hold the caves that first brought Fage here. The rock art is found in the highest of these caves, often painted on a very high ceiling. As Fage points out, "If something goes wrong, you die."

One large cave contains drawings of humans and animals, and around 350 images of **handprints,** some of them covered in patterns that look something like tattoos or body painting. Fage has counted 57 types of symbols depicted on the hands and is working hard to decode their meaning. Since the caves don't contain evidence of people living in them, it's likely that they were used for ceremonial or spiritual purposes. "We're dealing with **shamanistic** practices here . . . but I'm not sure what kind," says archaeologist Jean-Michel Chazine. The team thinks that the people who created these works of art more than 10,000 years ago may have been related to the aboriginal people of Australia.

Like cave paintings everywhere, the ones in Borneo are very **fragile,** and many of them may have already disappeared due to weather and time. The scientific community has learned about them only recently and is working to provide information that could lead to the protection of the rock art. Currently, Fage and Chazine display photos of the rock art and give information in French and English on their Web site, *www.kalimanthrope.com.* It's a place in cyberspace where anyone in the world can learn more about the mysterious caves of Kalimantan.

Sandstorm in Iraq

▲ Iceberg in the Atlantic Ocean

## Communication

**A** 🔁 Amazing photographs are easy to find on the Internet, but since images can be changed with computer software programs, you can't always believe what you see. Talk to a partner about these two pictures. Try to agree on which image is real and which is an example of *fauxtography*— a photograph that's designed to deceive the viewer.

## Writing

**A** Write a paragraph about each picture. Briefly describe the image, and then speculate about how the photograph was taken or changed to get the effect you see.

1. _____

   _____

   _____

   _____

2. _____

   _____

   _____

   _____

**B** 🔁 **GOAL CHECK** ✔ **Explain a mysterious image**

Take turns. Read your paragraphs to a partner. Try to agree on the best explanation for each image.

## Before You Watch

**A** 🔄 Discuss these questions. Is there any evidence that aliens from outer space visit Earth? How would they get here? What would they do here?

## While You Watch

**A** ▶️ Watch the video and complete each statement in the box to show the person's opinion.

**B** ▶️ Complete the video summary with words from the box. Then watch the video again and check your answers.

This video examines crop circles, a strange (1) _____ that occurs in England. These complex designs appear mysteriously in farmers' fields overnight, and people want to know if they're made by

(2) _____, such as you and me, or if the circles are

(3) _____ messages from aliens. To one researcher, crop

circles are a (4) _____—a mystery that he would like to solve. For one crop circle maker, on the other hand, there is no mystery. He thinks that artists and graphic designers make the crop circles using

wooden (5) _____ to flatten the grain and (6) _____ to help them create the designs.

1. **Reg Presley, Crop Circle Researcher:** Most crop circles are probably man-made, but

   _____

2. **Matthew, Crop Circle Maker:** Some people believe it's not possible for humans to make crop circles, but

   _____

| | |
|---|---|
| otherworldly | puzzle |
| boards | mortals |
| phenomenon | markers |

## After You Watch / Communication

**A** 🔄 Agree on some questions you would like to ask the crop circle makers. Think of questions for both alien and human crop circle makers. Then take turns answering them.

Students practicing handstands in China

## UNIT 11 GOALS

**1.** Talk about educational choices

**2.** Discuss your learning style

**3.** Talk about choosing a university major

**4.** Propose a new approach to teaching

135

## Vocabulary

**A** Read the article. Write the words in blue next to their meanings.

**Study Abroad Programs: SEA Semester**

For students who want to spend a semester away from their campus, the SEA Semester is a wonderful opportunity. Thirty-five students spend six weeks in Massachusetts, USA, taking courses about biology and the sea—and then use what they learn on a six-week trip on a small sailing ship, doing research with professional scientists. Each year, SEA Semester ships travel around the Atlantic and the Pacific. Students from colleges and universities in many countries enroll in the program. The tuition is not cheap—about $25,000—but scholarships are available. You don't have to have a science major, and sailing experience is not a requirement. You do have to apply very early, though—the deadline is six months before the program starts.

1. money given to good students to pay for their studies _____
2. main subject that you are studying _____
3. a series of lessons or lectures about a subject _____
4. the last day to do something _____
5. to fill out a form to ask for something _____
6. money you pay to study _____
7. an area of land with college or university buildings _____
8. something that is necessary _____
9. to join a school or a class _____
10. half of a school year _____

> I love the ocean.

> Yes, but six weeks is a long time on a small ship!

**B** 🗣 Discuss these questions with a partner. What are the good points and bad points of this program? Would you like to participate in this program? Why or why not?

## Grammar: *Should have, Would have,* and *Could have*

| | |
|---|---|
| Use modals with *have* + a past participle to imagine a different past. They are often used to talk about lost opportunities or possibilities. | Larry **should have applied** for a scholarship. (He didn't apply.)<br>Mary **couldn't have** enrolled sooner. (She enrolled as soon as possible.) |
| Use *should have* if something was advisable, or a good idea. | We **shouldn't have missed** the deadline. (We missed it. That wasn't a good idea.) |
| Use *could have* if something was possible. | I **could have read** the information more carefully. (I didn't read it carefully.) |
| Use *would have* if someone was willing to do something or if something was likely to happen. | They **would have given** you money. (They were willing, but you didn't ask.) |

**A** Complete the sentences. Use *should (not) have, could (not) have,* or *would (not) have* with a verb from the box.

| buy | help | give |
|---|---|---|
| practice | spend | like |

1. We _____ so much money last week. Now we don't have enough to pay the bills.

2. You didn't have to walk to the meeting. I _____ you a ride there.

3. Mike's mother is upset because he forgot her birthday. He had enough money, so he really _____ her a nice gift!

4. Andrew failed his driving test yesterday. He _____ more before he took the test.

5. Emma didn't apply to that school because she _____ living there. The town is really small and there's not much to do.

6. Tareq teaches calculus, so he _____ me with my homework. He didn't, however, because he thought I should figure the problems out myself.

**B** 🗣 Talk with your partner about the things in the box. Use *should have, could have,* or *would have.*

1. a bad decision that you made

2. an experience that you didn't try

> I could have lived in London for a year.

> Really!? Why didn't you go?

## Conversation

**A** 🔊 **21** Listen to the conversation with your book closed. Where does Josh want to study next year?

**Jamal:** Hi, Josh. What's up?

**Josh:** Not much. I have to study. I need to review 30 Japanese words for my quiz tomorrow, and they all look the same.

**Jamal:** You really picked a tough major!

**Josh:** The big problem is that I don't get many chances to speak the language. My college has a summer program in Tokyo. I should have applied for that.

**Jamal:** Why didn't you?

**Josh:** Because I missed the deadline! I could have spent two months in Japan. I would have studied 12 hours a day . . .

**Jamal:** Well, don't worry about it. I'm sure you'll have other chances.

**Josh:** Yeah, you're right. If I get good grades, there's an exchange program. I could spend next year at a Japanese university. I'm definitely going to apply.

**B** 🗣 Practice the conversation. Then have new conversations about your own experiences at school.

**C** 🗣 **GOAL CHECK** ✓ **Talk about educational choices**

Talk about how you chose the school you attend or the classes you are taking. How did you make the choices, and do you regret any of your decisions?

▲ A potter teaching someone to work with clay

## Listening

**A** Read the information in the chart below.

### Learning Styles

What is the best way to learn new information? One theory suggests that each person has a learning style they prefer. It proposes that there are four different kinds of learners.

| Auditory learners | Visual learners | Kinesthetic learners | Reading/Writing learners |
|---|---|---|---|
| prefer to get information by listening. They like to learn through lectures, group discussions, and conversations. | like to take in new information by seeing. Photos, charts, drawings, and diagrams help them to understand new ideas. | understand things best through experience and practice. They like to make things and use their bodies. | understand new information best when they read or write words. Using a textbook and reading articles are activities they prefer. |

Speaker 1: _____

Speaker 2: _____

Speaker 3: _____

**B** ◀)) 22 Listen to three speakers talk about their learning experiences. What did each person in the box study?

**C** ◀)) 22 Listen to the speakers again. What is each person's learning style?

| | | | | |
|---|---|---|---|---|
| **Speaker 1:** | auditory | visual | kinesthetic | reading/writing |
| **Speaker 2:** | auditory | visual | kinesthetic | reading/writing |
| **Speaker 3:** | auditory | visual | kinesthetic | reading/writing |

## Pronunciation: *Should have, Could have,* and *Would have*

**A** ◀)) 23 Listen to the sentences. Notice how the word *have* can be reduced to sound like /ə/ or /əv/.

1. I should have paid my tuition on time.

2. Marty shouldn't have chosen a science major.

3. We could have just stayed home.

4. I would have preferred to learn this by doing it.

**B** 🔁 Say these sentences to a partner. Use a reduced pronunciation, not a full pronunciation, of the word *have*.

1. Our teacher should have told us about the quiz.

2. He could have forgotten about the meeting.

3. I would have preferred to hear a lecture.

4. They could have studied in England last year.

5. She should have come to class that day.

6. The other instructor would have given a slide presentation.

## Communication

**A** 🔁 Give a partner this learning-style quiz. Read the questions to your partner, and circle his or her answers. Then check your partner's score.

1. If I don't know how to spell a word, I . . .

    **a.** pronounce it slowly.

    **b.** try to see the word in my mind.

    **c.** write it several ways and choose one.

    **d.** look it up in the dictionary.

2. If I need directions to a place, I like people to . . .

    **a.** tell me the directions.

    **b.** draw a map for me.

    **c.** take me there.

    **d.** write the directions for me.

3. If I have problems installing a new computer printer, I . . .

    **a.** call someone to ask questions.

    **b.** look for a diagram online.

    **c.** experiment until I figure it out.

    **d.** read the instructions.

4. I prefer classes that have lots of . . .

    **a.** lectures and discussion.

    **b.** pictures and diagrams.

    **c.** field trips and projects.

    **d.** books and reading.

5. When I study for a test, I like to . . .

    **a.** have someone ask me questions.

    **b.** look at charts and pictures.

    **c.** make flash cards and models.

    **d.** review my notes.

**Your score:** If you have three or more A answers, you are an auditory learner. If you have three or more B answers, you are a visual learner. If you have three or more C answers, you are a kinesthetic learner. If you have three or more D answers, you are a reading/writing learner.

**B** 🟶 Discuss these questions with two or three other students.

1. What was your preferred learning style from the quiz in exercise **A?**

2. Do you agree with the results of the quiz? Explain.

> I should have made a recording of my vocabulary words!

**C** 🔁 **GOAL CHECK** ✓ **Discuss your learning style**

What is the best way for you to learn these things: new vocabulary, an English grammar structure, reading and writing skills? Discuss ideas with your partner.

## Language Expansion: University majors

**A** University students are talking about their majors below. Read what they say, and write the major from the box.

1. I'm studying why some companies are so successful. **Major:** _business_

2. Our professor talked about why people have legal problems.

   **Major:** _____

3. I'm learning about how money systems work. **Major:** _____

4. Our class today was about where petroleum is found in the earth.

   **Major:** _____

5. In class, we talk about why some children learn more slowly.

   **Major:** _____

6. We study how we can help poor people. **Major:** _____

7. I had a lecture about where crops grow well in our country.

   **Major:** _____

8. I learn how I can help people with mental problems. **Major:** _____

9. We are studying how new chemicals are made in a laboratory.

   **Major:** _____

10. I've learned why some roads and bridges last for a long time.

    **Major:** _____

| | |
|---|---|
| economics | education |
| agriculture | law |
| business | engineering |
| psychology | chemistry |
| social work | geology |

**B** Discuss the questions with a partner.

1. What is your major? (or What will your major be?/What was your major?)

2. What are some things that people learn when they study that major?

3. Do you think it's better to choose a major because you enjoy it or because it will help you to get a good job?

> My major was history. I took a lot of courses about . . .

## Grammar: Noun clauses

| | |
|---|---|
| A noun clause can take the place of a noun in a sentence. | Do you remember <u>the reason</u>?<br>Do you remember **why she called**? |
| Make noun clauses with a *wh-* word, a subject, and a verb. | I don't know **when the deadline is.**<br>I'm interested in **how children learn.** |
| Noun clauses can be used in different parts of the sentence. | <u>Subject position</u>: **What you said** was very interesting.<br><u>Object position</u>: I liked **what you said.**<br><u>After a preposition</u>: I'll think about **what you said.** |

**A** Write answers with noun clauses.

1. Where are my keys?

   I don't know _where your keys are_____.

2. What did he talk about?

   I don't remember _____.

3. When is the lecture?

   Nobody told me _____.

4. Where does Katie live?

   I'm not really sure _____.

5. Why did John major in drama?

   I can't understand _____.

**B** 🔁 Take turns asking these questions. Use noun clauses in your answer. What are some things you're curious about? What was your favorite class last year? What did you learn about? What do you want to learn more about in the future?

> In history class, the teacher talked about how people lived in the past.

## Conversation

**A** 🔊 24 Listen to the conversation with your book closed. What two majors is Annie thinking about?

**Mike:** What's the matter, Annie? You look worried.

**Annie:** I guess I am. I just got a letter from the university, and it said the deadline for choosing my major is Friday.

**Mike:** You mean you still haven't decided?

**Annie:** It's so hard to make up my mind! Psychology is interesting because you learn why people do things. But if I studied agriculture, I would be able to help farmers produce more food.

**Mike:** Well, maybe you should think about what you do in class.

**Annie:** What do you mean?

**Mike:** You know, you don't like writing long papers, and a psychology major has to write tons of papers.

**Annie:** That's a good point. And I really like classes where I can use my knowledge of math and chemistry.

**Mike:** So it sounds like agriculture or maybe soil science are better options for you.

**Annie:** I think you're right.

**B** 🔁 Practice the conversation with a partner. Then make new conversations about the majors in the box.

**C** 🔁 **GOAL CHECK** ✔ **Talk about choosing a university major**

Think about two majors you are interested in. Why do you think they would be good for you? Why might they not be good? Discuss with a partner.

a. history and education

b. English and business

## GOAL 4: Propose a New Approach to Teaching

### Reading

**A** 🔄 What are the best ways to teach children? Check (✓) the items in the list.

_____ **1.** reading books

_____ **2.** writing information on the board

_____ **3.** doing research on the Internet

_____ **4.** showing them how to do things

_____ **5.** having them play and do experiments

**B** Read the text. Match the numbers with the correct information.

_____ **1.** 30

_____ **2.** 2006

_____ **3.** 12

_____ **4.** 80

_____ **5.** 2011

**a.** Tulley founded Tinkering School

**b.** target number of students at Brightworks for 2016

**c.** Tulley founded Brightworks School

**d.** highest grade at Brightworks School

**e.** number of students at Brightworks in its first year

**C** Complete the sentences.

1. Gever Tulley's background is in _____ .

2. By doing dangerous things, kids can learn how to be _____ .

3. Tulley founded the Tinkering School to let kids learn by _____ .

4. Students at Brightworks do _____ projects that build academic and social skills.

5. People who are comfortable taking _____ can make a big difference in the world.

**Gever Tulley** Tinkerer; Founder of the Tinkering School

# FIVE DANGEROUS THINGS (YOU SHOULD LET YOUR CHILDREN DO)

Gever Tulley is a man with a **mission.** He thinks that things like government safety regulations encourage modern parents to overprotect children, and that it is affecting their ability to learn and think. He wants kids to do dangerous things. In fact, he even wrote a book called *Fifty Dangerous Things (You Should Let Your Children Do)* to encourage parents to allow their children to experiment—safely—with fire, pocket knives, and power tools. He thinks they should lick nine-volt batteries and take appliances apart, among many other activities that might seem a little dangerous, at least to their parents.

This might sound crazy, but Tulley is serious. He argues that children who experiment and explore their world learn about natural phenomena, develop attention and concentration skills, and understand how complicated systems work. He thinks that activities like throwing a spear can even help children's brains develop more fully and improve their skills in visualization and prediction. Most importantly, Tulley says, his goals behind encouraging kids to take risks is promoting "safety and [...] simple things that we can do to raise our kids to be creative, confident and in control of the environment around them." Tulley wants parents and kids to do these activities together, but with kids taking the lead.

Gever Tulley knows a lot about taking risks. Although his **background** is in computer science, he has developed programs to help children have the kind of experiences he **advocates** in his book. First, in 2006, he started the **Tinkering** School, a summer camp

"... As the boundaries of what we determine as the safety zone grow ever smaller, we cut off our children from valuable opportunities to learn how to interact with the world around them."

Gever Tulley's idea worth spreading is that we should let kids take more risks. Watch Tulley's full TED Talk on TED.com.

where "kids learn how to build the things they think of." Kids at Tinkering School have built a treehouse, a bridge, and lots of boats and vehicles.

After that risk, Tulley took an even bigger one. In 2011, he and a colleague, Bryan Welch, started a school in San Francisco, California, called Brightworks. From its first class of 11 students, the school has grown to 30 students, and there are plans to **enroll** 80 students by 2016. Students at Brightworks learn through doing group projects that build their academic and social skills, at the same time as they grow as community members.

Just imagine what kind of risks these kids will take as adults and the changes they will create in the world around them. Why not take a risk yourself?

**mission**  a task or job that someone is given to do
**background**  the experiences, knowledge, education, etc., in a person's past
**advocate**  a person who argues for or supports a cause or policy
**tinker**  to try to repair or improve something (such as a machine) by making small changes or adjustments to it
**enroll**  to join as a member or participant

The old ways of learning don't work anymore. In the past, schools often taught children through memorization. They (1) _____ had the chance to play and experiment more. For example, in a biology class, students (2) _____ grown plants or they (3) _____ raised small animals. This way, they (4) _____ learned about the life cycle. Their parents and teachers (5) _____ let them take risks—that's how people make big discoveries and changes.

## Communication

**A** 🔁 Discuss the questions with a partner. Which ways of teaching do you think work best with the subjects in the box?

art    biology    history    computer science    literature    mathematics

## Writing

**A** Complete the conversation with noun clauses.

**Martha:** You want to be a teacher, don't you? What subject are you going to teach?

**Juan:** I'm not sure (1) _____. Math interests me a lot, but I'm better at science. What do you think I should choose?

**Martha:** Oh, I have no idea (2) _____!

**Juan:** Well, I have some time to decide. Who was your favorite teacher when you were a child?

**Martha:** I don't remember (3) _____. It seems like a long time ago! Maybe Mrs. Jackson, my music teacher. . . We made a lot of noise in that class.

**B** Complete the opinion paragraph in the box with *should have, could have,* or *would have.*

**C** Write an opinion paragraph about new approaches to teaching. Be sure to use *should have, could have,* or *would have.*

**D** 🔁 | **GOAL CHECK** ✓ Propose a new approach to teaching

Share your ideas about approaches to learning. Which approaches do you think would be most successful? What are your reasons?

England, U.K.

## Before You Watch

**A** 🔁 Discuss these questions with a partner. Which country had butlers in the past? Where did butlers work? What did they do? Have you ever seen a butler in a movie or TV show? Describe the character.

## While You Watch

**A** ▶️ Watch the video *Butler School* and circle the answers.

1. The students come from ( the same | many ) countries.

2. The students think the course is ( difficult | fun ).

3. The students learn to be a butler by ( practicing | reading ).

**B** ▶️ Watch again and circle the things students study at this school.

| | | |
|---|---|---|
| 1. how to walk correctly | 4. how to drive a car | 7. how to stop a thief |
| 2. what to say to a king | 5. how to cook expensive food | 8. how to speak English |
| 3. what to say on the telephone | 6. how to iron a newspaper | |

## After You Watch / Communication

**A** 🔁 Role-play the situations in the box.

**B** 👥 Make a magazine advertisement for a butler school. Include information on a butler's work, what students will learn at the school, and why being a butler is a good job. Decorate your ad with drawings.

**Student A:** You are a wealthy professional who needs a butler.

**Student B:** You have graduated from butler school, and you are applying for a job.

# Space

A new Japanese island, named Niijima,
merging with the island of Nishinoshima

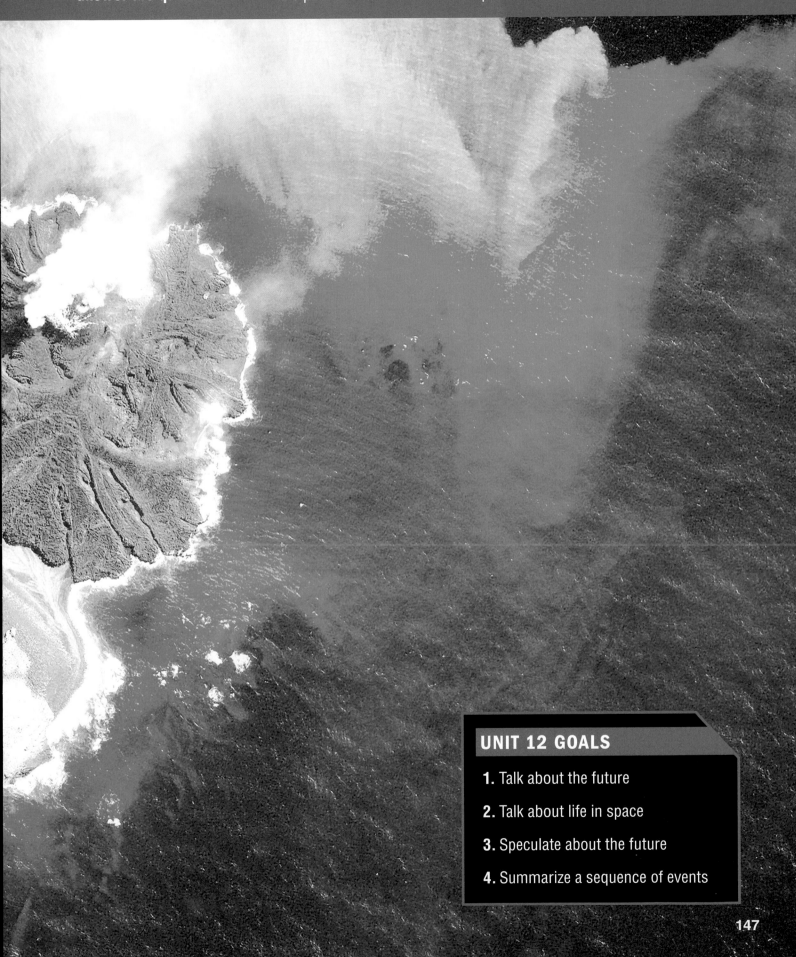

### UNIT 12 GOALS

**1.** Talk about the future

**2.** Talk about life in space

**3.** Speculate about the future

**4.** Summarize a sequence of events

▲ Astronaut Edwin Aldrin walks on the Moon.

## Vocabulary

**A** Read the article. Notice the words in blue.

**Space Exploration**

The space age began in 1957, when Russia put the satellite *Sputnik* into orbit around the earth. Since that time, human beings have explored the solar system with manned missions to the moon and unmanned spacecrafts to Mars, Jupiter, and other planets. Closer to Earth, working on board the space station has taught us much about people's ability to live in space. This knowledge has changed some people's ideas about human beings colonizing the moon or Mars, while others continue to dream about this possibility.

**B** Write the words in blue next to their meaning. There are two phrases.

1. with people on board _____

2. the sun, moon, and planets _____

3. vehicle designed to travel or stay in space _____

4. without people on board _____

5. natural objects such as Earth or Saturn _____

6. man-made space object for communication or collecting information_____

7. curved path in space around a planet, moon, or star _____

8. the act of populating a new place, such as the moon _____

9. special journeys or tasks _____

10. spacecraft on which people live and do scientific work for weeks or months at a time _____

## Grammar: Talking about the future

| Use *will* or *be going to* + verb to talk about the future.<br>Also use *will* + verb to decide something suddenly. | Space exploration **will/is going to** be even more international in the future.<br><br>Is that tea? **I'll** have some, please. |
| --- | --- |
| Use the present continuous tense to talk about definite future plans. | Joyce and Walter **are flying** to Mexico City next month. |
| Use the simple present tense to talk about scheduled events in the future. | Our train **leaves** at 8:30 a.m.<br>The movie **starts** in five minutes. |

**A** Read this message from a student to her former teacher. Underline the expressions that refer to the future.

Dear Mr. Taylor,

I hope you're doing well, and I hope you have a few minutes to read the attached document. It's a story that I'm writing about a brother and sister in the future. The year is 2025, and the brother is going to be part of a manned mission to Mars. He's going there on a spacecraft that leaves the next day. The sister is a photographer, and she plans to take pictures of the launch. The conflict in the story occurs when the brother feels very sick after dinner. They decide that the sister will pretend to be him, and she will take his place on the mission to Mars. If you don't mind, I'd really like to hear your opinion of the story.

Thanks very much,
Roberta Battaglia

**B** 🔁 Work with a partner. What will these be like in the future? Make predictions with *be going to* and *will* about the topics in the box.

> transportation   the environment   communication   food

## Conversation

**A** 🔊 **25** Close your book and listen to the conversation. When does the training program start?

**Tina:** Alex, what are you going to do after high school?
**Alex:** Whoa! I don't even know what I'm doing after school today!
**Tina:** Very funny. I'm going to enroll in a training program.
**Alex:** What kind of training program?
**Tina:** They teach you to be a laboratory assistant. It doesn't take very long, and it starts a week after graduation.
**Alex:** That sounds all right. And what will you do when you finish the program?
**Tina:** I'll look for a job in a scientific laboratory. All of them need lab assistants.
**Alex:** That's a pretty good idea. Eric is joining the military when he graduates.
**Tina:** So everybody has a plan except you.
**Alex:** True. That's what I'll do after school today! I'll plan my future!

**B** 🔁 Practice the conversation with a partner. Switch roles and practice it again.

**C** 🔁 **GOAL CHECK** ✅ **Talk about the future**

Think about your own future. Tell your partner what you will probably do in:

- the immediate future (this afternoon, tonight, tomorrow).
- the near future (next month, next year, after you graduate).
- the more distant future (in five years, in ten years, when you retire).

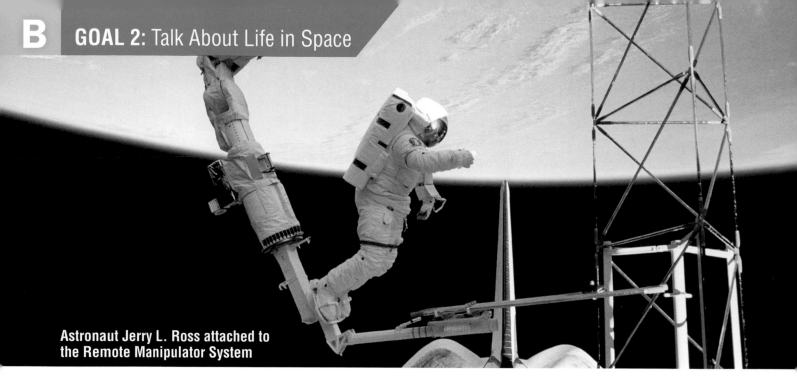

Astronaut Jerry L. Ross attached to
the Remote Manipulator System

## Listening

**A** 🔊 **26** Listen to a radio interview with an astronaut. Check (✓) the things she has done.

☐ studied botany (the science of plants)

☐ conducted experiments on board the International Space Station

☐ made repairs outside the International Space Station

☐ slept attached to a wall of the International Space Station

☐ returned to Earth

**B** 🔊 **26** Listen again and complete the chart.

| | |
|---|---|
| **Plants involved in Wilma Foster's experiments:** | |
| **Exciting aspects of life on board the International Space Station:** | |
| **Difficult aspects of life on board the International Space Station:** | |

### Engage!

Why do some people enjoy exploring extreme places such as space, high mountains, or deep parts of the ocean?

**C** 💬 Discuss these questions with a partner.

1. Why do you think Dr. Foster wants to return to the International Space Station?

2. Why are the results of experiments conducted in space important?

## Pronunciation: Stress in compound nouns

**A** 🔊 **27** Listen to and repeat the words. Notice how the stress is on the first part of each compound noun.

> spacecraft   backpack   lifesaver   hardware   bedroom

**B** 🔊 **28** Some compound nouns are written as two words, and some are hyphenated. Listen to and repeat the words.

> space walk   fruit juice   space station   follow-up   check-in

**C** 🔁 Fill in each blank with a compound noun from exercises **A** and **B**. Then compare your answers with a partner's, and take turns reading the sentences aloud.

1. I'm thirsty! Do we have any _____?

2. The _____ orbits the Earth.

3. That study guide was a real _____! I might not have passed the exam without it.

4. I think it would be difficult to sleep without a _____.

5. After you arrive at the hotel, you will need to _____ at the desk.

6. Hector left his _____ at home, and all his books were in it!

## Communication

**A** 👥 Imagine that your group is going to be part of a mission to the International Space Station. Research the experiments done there. What kind of experiments will your group do? Then make a list of everything you will need to take on board the space station in order to conduct your experiments.

**B** 👥 Do a short presentation for the class. Talk about your plans for the space station mission, and explain the items on your list.

**C** 🔁 **GOAL CHECK** ✓ **Talk about life in space**

Would you enjoy living and working aboard the International Space Station? Explain to a partner why you would or would not want to be an astronaut.

▲ Astronaut Kathryn Sullivan looks at the Earth from the Challenger

Word Focus

Scientists **conduct experiments.**

**Speaker A**

in a little while
one day
in ten years

**Speaker B**

someday soon
one of these days
sooner or later

## Language Expansion: Future time expressions

**A** 🔊 **29**  Listen to two university professors. Underline the time expressions on the left when you hear them.

**B** 🔊 **29**  Listen again to Speaker A, and make a simple time line. Which event happens the soonest? Which happens in the more distant future?

**C** 🔊 **29**  Listen again to Speaker B. Which two events is the speaker less certain about? Which event is she more certain about? How do you know?

## Grammar: Modals and modal-like phrases to talk about the future

| | |
|---|---|
| Use the modals *may*, *might*, and *could* + a verb to express a future possibility or to speculate about the future. | She **may** teach part-time next year. The launch **might not** be delayed this time. All of this **could** happen within our lifetime. |
| Use modal-like phrases to express ability or necessity in the future. | I **am not going to be able to** call you tomorrow. Scientists **will have to** solve this problem someday soon. |
| Do not use single-word modals with *will* or *be going to*. | People **will** (~~can~~) **be able to** live on Mars someday. Sherry **is going to** (~~must~~) **have to** take Physics 322 sooner or later. |

**A** Fill in the blank with any appropriate expression from the chart. Not all items need an expression.

1. In the near future, people will _____ live longer than they can now.

2. More women _____ run for president in future elections.

3. I'm sure I'm going to _____ pay a lot for the jacket I want.

4. Do you think people _____ live on the moon someday?

5. The space station (not) _____ stay in orbit forever.

**B** Answer the questions in your notebook using expressions from the chart.

1. What do you think people will be wearing in 2050?

2. What do you think transportation will be like in 20 years?

3. When do you think people will be able to travel to Mars?

4. What do you think people are going to need to take to Mars?

5. What kinds of new jobs do you think there will be in the future?

**C** Take turns asking the questions and sharing your answers from exercise **B**.

## Conversation

**A** 🔊 30 Close your book and listen to the conversation. Which speaker is the most convincing to you?

**Jacob:** What do you think? Will people ever walk on the moon again?

**Matthew:** I don't know. They might, but there are still problems with the technology.

**Jacob:** Do you mean the space shuttle accidents?

**Matthew:** Of course. It's risky to send people into space.

**Jacob:** That's true, but it's the only way to experience the moon firsthand.

**Matthew:** Sure, but unmanned spacecraft can travel much farther than the moon.

**Jacob:** And there are going to be technical problems with those missions, too.

**Matthew:** OK, any future space exploration could have technical problems.

**Jacob:** But a human being could repair equipment and solve problems!

**Matthew:** You're right. Maybe I'll get lucky and they'll send you into space.

**B** Practice the conversation with a partner. Switch roles and practice it again.

**C** **GOAL CHECK** ✓ **Speculate about the future**

Talk in a small group. Do you know about any space exploration that is happening now? What parts of space do you think people will travel to or explore in the near future and in the distant future?

## Reading

**A** How quickly can you find the answers in the article?

1. Why is Earth's atmosphere a problem for astronomers? _____

2. What did Lyman Spitzer propose? _____

3. What kind of object was Shoemaker-Levy 9? _____

4. When was the final Hubble service mission completed? _____

**B** Circle **T** for *true*, **F** for *false*, or **NI** for *no information* (if the answer is not in the reading).

1. The best telescopes on Earth are not affected by the atmosphere.　　**T　F　NI**

2. Lyman Spitzer was Russian.　**T　F　NI**

3. Spitzer thought the orbiting telescope would mainly add to the scientific ideas that already existed.　　**T　F　NI**

4. Hubble has confirmed that black holes really exist.　　**T　F　NI**

5. The universe is expanding more quickly than it used to.　**T　F　NI**

**C** 🔁 The reading passage is organized in chronological order. With a partner, discuss what the article says about telescopes in the past, present, and future.

### Word Focus

**supplement** = add to
**modify** = change
**expanding** = becoming larger; moving outward
**acceleration** = moving faster

Space

# THE HUBBLE SPACE TELESCOPE

For centuries, astronomers looking at the moon, the planets, and the stars have faced a basic problem: the earth's atmosphere. Although it provides the air we breathe as well as protection from the sun, the atmosphere prevents us from seeing clearly into space—even with the largest and most advanced telescopes.

Then came Lyman Spitzer, an astrophysicist with a remarkable idea: put a large telescope in orbit around the earth, *outside* of the earth's atmosphere. Spitzer suggested this idea in 1946, eleven years before Russia launched the world's first man-made satellite and long before technology such as digital imaging or the space shuttle existed. Spitzer said the telescope would not only test existing ideas, but also inspire completely new ones. "The chief contribution of such a radically new and more powerful instrument," he predicted, "would be, not to **supplement** our present ideas of the universe we live in, but rather to uncover new phenomena not yet imagined, and perhaps to **modify** profoundly our basic concepts of space and time."

Spitzer was right. In 1993, NASA released the first images from the Hubble telescope. Since then, scientists have used Hubble to follow the comet Shoemaker-Levy 9 as it hit the giant planet Jupiter. They have produced images of the amazing and unique beauty of planetary nebulae—giant clouds of gas produced by dying stars. They have proved the existence of black holes at the centers of galaxies. And just as Spitzer predicted, Hubble has provided new information that has changed our ideas about the universe.

Astronomers already knew that the universe was **expanding,** but they expected this expansion to be slowing down due to the gravity of all the material in the universe, just as a ball thrown into the air falls back to Earth. Instead, astronomers discovered that the expansion is not slowing down at all—it is speeding up! It is as if a ball thrown into the air at first slowed, but then sped up and simply flew away. No natural force on Earth can do this, but some kind of energy must be causing the **acceleration.**

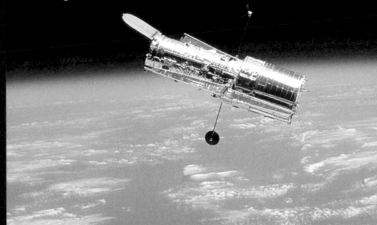

**The Hubble telescope orbiting Earth**

Scientists are calling this unknown force *dark energy* and are working to learn more about it. However, Hubble is getting old, and its final scheduled service mission was completed in 2009. Fortunately, other orbiting telescopes such as the Spitzer Space Telescope and the Chandra X-ray Observatory are sending information to Earth, and the gigantic James Webb Space Telescope is scheduled for launch in the near future. Together with a network of telescopes on the ground, these space observatories promise, as Lyman Spitzer said back in 1946, to change not only what we know, but also how we learn.

**The Orinon Nebula**

# GOAL 4: Summarize a Sequence of Events

**Technology tracks route for a tourist**

Technology developed by space programs:

- artificial heart pumps
- weather satellites
- liquid-cooled garments to treat injuries
- robotic arm to assist in surgeries
- global positioning systems (GPS)
- technology for cleaning polluted land or water
- protective material for metal bridges

## Writing Strategy

A thesis statement is often at the end of the introduction. Your thesis statement must:
- Make a claim that someone could disagree with.
- Provide a preview of your ideas.

## Communication

**A** Read the information in the box. Discuss which kinds of technology could benefit you or someone you know.

**B** As you know, space exploration is extremely expensive. Make a list of other kinds of programs governments could spend money on in order to help people.

## Writing

**A** Write a three-paragraph composition with an introduction, a body paragraph, and a conclusion. In your composition, answer the following questions:

- In what ways does space exploration benefit human beings?

- Do those benefits outweigh the costs of space exploration?

**B** Exchange compositions. Read your partner's composition carefully, and write answers to the questions.

1. Introduction: Does it give background information about space exploration?

2. Thesis statement: Does it make a claim and express a clear point of view?

3. Thesis statement: Does it give the reader a preview of the writer's main points?

4. Body paragraph: Does it give enough reasons and examples to support the thesis statement?

**C** Talk with your partner about your answers to the questions above.

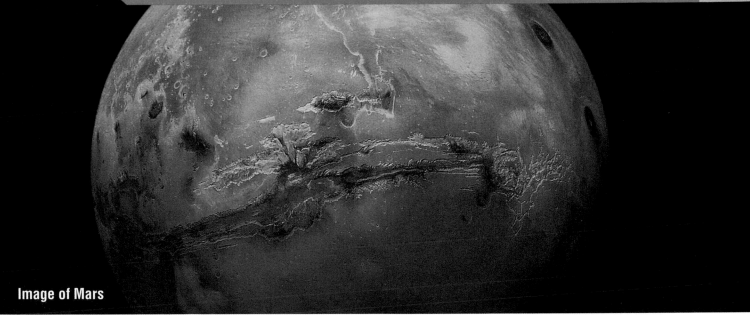

Image of Mars

## Before You Watch

**A** Read about the Curiosity rover. Use a dictionary to help you with the words in **bold.**

## While You Watch

**A** ▶ Number the steps in the order they happen.

_____ Launch      _____ Testing      _____ Touchdown      _____ Cruise

**B** ▶ Write answers to these questions in your notebook.

1. How many Americans were watching when the Curiosity rover landed on Mars?

2. How many minutes does it take for information from Mars to reach Earth?

3. When people on Earth learn that the spacecraft is at the top of Mars's atmosphere, how many minutes has the rover been on the planet's surface?

4. What role does the computer play in the Entry, Descent, and Landing?

## After You Watch / Communication

**A** Discuss the quotations from the video. What do you think the speakers mean?

1. Adam Steltzner: "It is the result of reasoned engineering thought, but it still looks crazy."

2. Tom Rivellini: "Entry, Descent, and Landing, also known as EDL, is referred to as the "seven minutes of terror . . . If any one thing doesn't work just right, it's game over."

> A vehicle called a "rover" has been sent to Mars to study the planet's rocks and soil, but getting it there wasn't the most difficult part. In the seven minutes called "Entry, **Descent**, and Landing," a **parachute** helped to **decelerate** the spacecraft from 13,000 miles per hour down to zero. Then, a special vehicle called the "sky **crane**" lowered the rover to the **surface** of Mars and flew away!

# TEDTALKS

**Bill Stone** Engineer and Explorer
# I'M GOING TO THE MOON. WHO'S WITH ME?

## Before You Watch

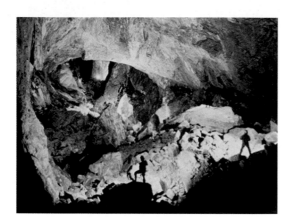

**A** Look at the picture and answer the questions with a partner.

**1.** Where are these people?

**2.** What are they doing?

**3.** Would you be comfortable in a place like this? Why or why not?

**B** Engineer Bill Stone has explored deep caves like this one. Here are some words you will hear in his TED Talk. Complete the paragraph with the correct words. Not all words will be used.

> **abyss** *n.* a hole so deep or a space so great that it cannot be measured
> **chamber** *n.* a space inside something else
> **expedition** *n.* a journey, especially by a group of people for a specific purpose (such as to explore a distant place or to do research)
> **illuminated** *adj.* lit by bright lights
> **obsolete** *adj.* no longer used because something newer exists
> **remoteness** *n.* the state of being far away or distant

Bill Stone has led many (1) _____ to some of the deepest caves on earth. In order to go down into a deep (2) _____, he has developed new devices and technology. He and his teams camp below ground in places that are wet, cold, and not (3) _____ at all. Now he wants to explore the moon. He says that our old ways of thinking about travel to the moon are (4) _____. Despite its (5) _____, Stone believes that it is possible for people to live on the moon and to access its resources.

**C** Look at the pictures on the next page. Check (✓) the information that you predict you will hear in the TED Talk.

_____ **1.** When you explore a cave, you often find underground water.

_____ **2.** It is possible for human beings to live and work on the moon.

_____ **3.** We still don't know much about space travel.

## While You Watch

**A** Watch the TED Talk. Circle the main idea.

**1.** If we are going to explore underground, underwater, and in space, we need to leave old ideas behind.

**2.** It is very dangerous to be an extreme explorer because of underground water in caves.

**3.** We need to explore the moon and outer space more than we already have.

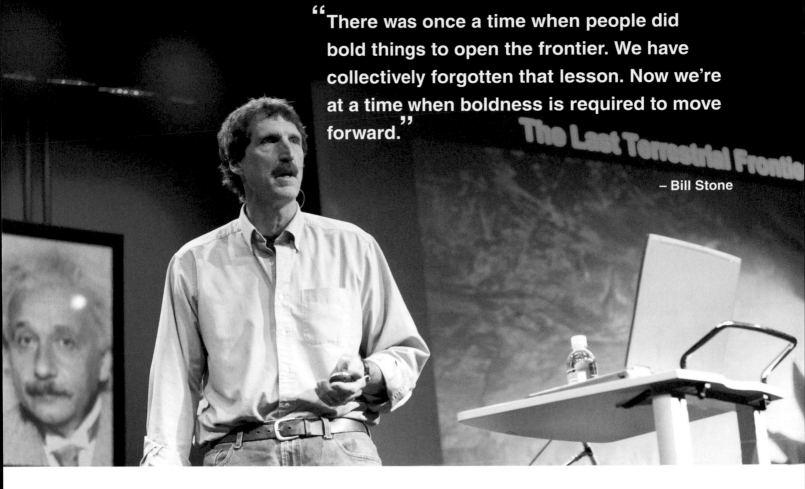

"There was once a time when people did bold things to open the frontier. We have collectively forgotten that lesson. Now we're at a time when boldness is required to move forward."

*The Last Terrestrial Frontier*

– Bill Stone

**B** ▶ The photos below relate to the ideas in the TED Talk. Watch the talk again, and write the letter of the caption under the correct photo.

**a.** Bill Stone thinks there will be commercial travel to the moon in the future.

**b.** When Stone's teams explore deep caves, they make camp in one of its chambers.

**c.** Humans may live on the moon in order to access its resources.

**d.** There is often a great deal of water in very deep caves.

1. ___

2. ___

3. ___

4. ___

**Challenge!** Read Stone's speaker profile on TED.com to learn more about the incredible places he's been. Which one would you most like to visit? What questions would you ask Stone about his experiences as an explorer? Share your ideas with a partner.

# **TED**TALKS

## After You Watch

caves   companies   darkness
devices   imagination

**A** Complete the summary with the words in the box.

Bill Stone has gone into some of the world's deepest (1) _____,
and in order to learn more about the world below, he has developed
(2) _____ that can map huge chambers in complete
(3) _____. Now he has turned his (4) _____ to the
moon. Stone wants to see private (5) _____ build settlements
on the moon so they can look for minerals and other resources.

**B** Match the phrases to complete sentences from the TED Talk.

**Cause**

1. ____ Stone's cave exploration teams have had
2. ____ A space vehicle's fuel can equal
3. ____ NASA would like to return to the moon by
4. ____ One of Stone's devices can help an explorer breathe
5. ____ Europa, one of Jupiter's moons, has ice that is

**Effect**

a. at 200 meters under water.
b. 16 miles thick.
c. as many as 150 members.
d. 90% of its weight.
e. the year 2024.

**C** Read the statements below. Circle the ones that paraphrase Bill Stone's ideas.

1. It is now possible to explore deep underground without too many problems.
2. When you are designing new equipment to go underwater, you need to think about possible dangers.
3. Going to the moon in the same way as before will help us learn new things about space.
4. It is a good idea to let private companies explore the moon.

# Project

Bill Stone wants to build a base on the moon and allow private companies to access its resources. Has Stone convinced you that this is a good idea? Use his ideas to write a letter for or against industrial exploration.

**A** 🔁 Work with a partner to find facts and opinions from the talk you can include.

**B** 🔁 Decide with your partner which facts and opinions from exercise **A** to include. Choose the ones that support your idea the best.

**C** 🔁 Write your letter. Show your letter to a different partner. Is your opinion easy to understand? Does he or she have ideas for improvement?

> To the Editor:
>
> I am writing to _____ .
>
> In my opinion, _____ . If we don't _____ , we will _____ .
>
> It is also important to _____ . We will _____ if we _____ .
>
> Finally, I think _____ . If _____ , then _____ .
>
> Yours sincerely,
>
> _____

**Challenge!** Bill Stone gave his TED Talk in 2007. Is Stone still working on this idea? How have industrial and commercial space exploration advanced since then?

# GLOSSARY

## UNIT 1 PEOPLE AND PLACES

**ancient:** very old; from an earlier time

**arid:** describes places that receive very little rain

**employment:** having a job

**fishing:** catching fish

**frigid:** describes extremely cold places

**herding:** caring for a group of animals such as cattle or sheep

**hunting:** killing wild animals for food

**inhabit:** to live in a place

**migration:** moving from one part of the world to another

**occur:** to happen

**political:** relating to the way power is achieved or used in a society

**rainy:** describes places that receive a large amount of rain

**sail:** to move across water in a boat using the wind

**snowy:** describes places that receive a large amount of snow

**temperate:** describes places with distinct seasons that are never extremely hot or cold

**tropical:** describes hot, humid places near the earth's equator

## UNIT 2 THE MIND

**cell:** the smallest part of an animal or plant

**concentrate:** think very hard about something

**conclusion:** something you decide after looking at all the information

**conduct:** to organize and carry something out

**experiment:** a scientific test to see if something is true

**hearing:** your ability to sense sounds

**laboratory:** a place where scientists work

**landmark:** something easily seen, such as a tall building or a mountain

**memorize:** learn so that you can remember exactly

**memory:** your ability to remember things

**mental:** in your mind

**participate:** to take part in an activity or event

**portion:** part

**practice:** to do something repeatedly in order to perfect it

**react:** speak or move when something happens

**recall:** to remember

**research:** studying something to discover new facts about it

**results:** the information that scientists get after an experiment

**retain:** keep, continue to have

**sight:** your ability to see

**smell:** your ability to sense the odor of things

**survey:** collecting information by asking many people the same questions

**taste:** your ability to sense the flavor of things

**technique:** a way to do an activity

**theory:** a scientific idea

**touch:** your ability to sense how things feel

**visualize:** make a picture in your mind

## UNIT 3 CHANGING PLANET

**climate change:** a change in the normal weather patterns

**coal:** a black mineral made of carbon taken from the ground

**conservation:** saving and protecting the environment

**deforestation:** the cutting down of trees over a large area

**drought:** a time of little or no rainfall

**extreme:** very great in degree or intensity

**global warming:** a gradual rise in the earth's temperature

**increase:** the number, level, or amount becoming greater

**invasive species:** plants and animals with no local natural controls on their populations

**led to:** caused

**oil:** a thick liquid found underground and used as a fuel

**sea level:** the average level of the ocean

**temperature:** how hot or cold something is

## UNIT 4 MONEY

**ATM:** automatic teller machine (a machine that dispenses money)

**avoid:** to stay away from

**bargain:** something good for a low price

**borrow:** get money that you will give back in the future

**budget:** a plan for spending your money

**cash:** money in coins and bills

**checking account:** a bank account that you write checks from

**decide:** to reach a conclusion

**deposit:** put money into a bank

**expenses:** money that you spend

**hope:** faith that a situation will improve

**in debt:** owing money to a bank or a company

**income:** money that you receive for working

**lend:** give money to another person that they will give back in the future

**love:** to like with great intensity

**PIN number:** personal identification number (secret number)

**receipt:** a paper that shows how much money you have paid or given

**savings account:** a bank account where you save money to spend later

**stop:** to end a movement or activity

**teller:** a person who works in a bank

**withdraw:** take money out of the bank

## UNIT 5 SURVIVAL

**banned:** not allowed

**cope:** deal with something successfully

**ecosystem:** all the plants and animals in a certain area

**emergency:** a bad situation that requires immediate attention

**endangered:** with species, describes one that might become extinct soon

**equipment:** items needed for a purpose

**evacuate:** to leave a place because it has become dangerous

**first aid:** emergency medical treatment

**natural disaster:** earthquakes, floods, or other damaging natural events

**panic:** uncontrolled fear in response to danger

**predatory:** describes an animal that eats other animals

**preparation:** the process of getting ready

**preservation:** keeping or maintaining something

**reserve:** a place where hunting and fishing are not allowed

**restore:** to return something to the way it was before

**situation:** the way things are at a certain time

**species:** a certain kind of plant or animal

**supplies:** food, equipment, and other things people need

## UNIT 6 ART

**abstract:** describes art made with shapes and lines, not pictures of real things

**aware:** conscious of, alert to

**bronze:** a gray to reddish-brown metal made of tin and copper

**clay:** a material made from earth

**depict:** to describe or portray something through art

**diverse:** varied, different from each other

**express:** show what you think or feel about something

**glass:** a hard transparent material used in windows, buildings, ornaments, and other objects

**leather:** a material made from animal skin

**painting:** a work of art made with paint

**realistic:** describes art that looks like real things

**represent:** be a symbol for something

**sculpture:** a work of art made by carving stone, metal, or wood

**silver:** a white, shinny, metallic element used for making jewelry, knives, forks spoons, and other objects

**stained glass:** a work of art made with pieces of colored glass

**stone:** a hard material found in the ground

**style:** a way of making art that is used by one artist, or a small group

**technique:** a particular way to do or make something

**textile:** a cloth or fabric made by weaving

**wood:** a material made from trees

## UNIT 7 GETTING AROUND

**board:** get on a plane, bus, or ship

**connect:** come together

**destination:** the place you are going to

**directly:** without stopping or changing direction

**efficient:** not using too much time or energy

**fare:** money you pay to use public transportation

**fuel:** a substance like gasoline or oil that is burned to give power

**increase:** become greater in number or amount

**pass:** a card that shows you have paid to use public transportation for a period of time

**passengers:** a person who is traveling in a vehicle

**reduce:** make smaller

**route:** the way that a train or bus usually goes

**speed:** how fast something moves

**terminal:** the end of a train or bus route

**ticket:** a paper that shows you have paid to use public transportation

**transfer:** change from one route to another

**vehicle:** a car, truck, or bus

## UNIT 8 COMPETITION

**advice:** an opinion or opinions given to someone about what to do

**athlete:** a person who plays sports

**championship:** a competition to find the best player or team in a sport

**coach:** someone who trains a person or a sports team

**competitive:** a situation of competition where something tries to be as good or better than something else

**diet:** a weight loss program

**game:** an activity or sport, often with rules, that people play

**individual:** one person

**lose:** to be defeated by another person or team

**match:** a competition such as a soccer match or tennis match

**medal:** a metal disk given as a prize in a sports event

**points:** the numbers that are added together to give the score

**schedule:** a list of timed, planned activities or events

**score:** the total number of points a player or team receives in a sports event

**scoreboard:** a large sign that shows the score during a sports event

**sportsmanship:** polite behavior during a sports event

**team:** a group of people who compete together

**training:** learning and practicing a sport

**trophy:** a prize such as a cup given to the winner of a competition

**win:** to score more points than another person or team

## UNIT 9 DANGER

**ambulance:** a vehicle used to bring sick or injured people to a hospital

**emergency room:** part of a hospital that takes care of sick or injured people who need immediate attention

**estimate:** guess about the number or amount of something

**fire department:** the organization responsible for putting out unwanted fires in a town or city

**hospital:** a medical institution that gives health care for sick or injured people

**injured:** hurt a person's body

**pharmacy:** a drugstore

**poison:** something that kills people if they eat or drink it

**police:** a part of the government whose men and women in uniform prevent crimes, enforce the law, and catch criminals

**prevent:** make sure that something doesn't happen

**risk:** possibility that something bad will happen

**substance:** a solid, liquid, or gas

**survive:** live through a dangerous situation

**toxic:** containing poison

## UNIT 10 MYSTERIES

**carve:** to shape something by cutting it artistically and exactly

**construct:** to build, make, or create something

**evidence:** clues that make you believe something is true

**figure out:** to solve or understand something

**investigate:** to try to find out what happened or what is true

**massive:** something that is huge in size or quantity

**prehistoric:** describes people or things that existed before information was written down

**remains:** the parts of something that are left after most of it is gone

**reveal:** to uncover something hidden

**speculate:** to make guesses about something

## UNIT 11 LEARNING

**art:** the study of art, its history and its application

**agriculture:** the study of farming

**apply:** fill out a form to ask for something

**biology:** the science and study of life

**business:** the study of how companies work

**campus:** an area of land with college or university buildings

**chemistry:** the science of substances and how they react together

**computer science:** the study computers and their use

**course:** a series of lessons or lectures about a subject

**deadline:** the last day to do something

**economics:** the study of money

**education:** the study of ways to teach and learn

**engineering:** the study of how to build and make things

**enroll:** join a school or a class

**geology:** the science of earth and rocks

**history:** the study of past events, including people and civilizations

**law:** the study of how laws work

**lecture:** a speech

**literature:** the study of written works, such as novels, poems, and plays

**major:** main subject that you are studying

**mathematics:** the study of numbers, symbols, and forms that follow strict rules and laws

**psychology:** the science of the mind

**requirement:** something that you must have or do to be suitable for something

**scholarship:** money given to good students to pay for their studies

**semester:** half of a school year

**social work:** the study of how to give help and advice to people with social problems

**tuition:** money you pay to study

## UNIT 12 SPACE

**astronaut:** a person who goes into outer space

**colonize:** the act of populating a new place such as the Moon

**communication:** the act of passing on information

**environment:** the air, land, water, and surroundings that people, plants, and animals live in

**exploration:** the process of exploring; looking for new things

**food:** something that can be eaten that nourishes

**launch:** to send up into the air

**manned:** with people on board

**mission:** a special journey or task

**orbit:** a curved path in space around a planet, moon, or star

**planet:** a large object such as Earth or Saturn that moves around a star

**satellite:** a man-made object in space that moves around Earth

**solar system:** the Sun, Earth, planets, moons, etc., that move around the Sun

**spacecraft:** a vehicle that flies in space

**space station:** a space craft that can support manned operations in space

**transportation:** ways to move from one place to another

**universe:** the whole of space and all the planets, stars, etc.

**unmanned:** without people on board

## GRAMMAR

adjectives
    objective clauses, 100–101
    *so* + adjective + *that,* 8–9
    subjective clauses, 72–73
adverbs
    clauses of time, 112
indirect questions, 88–89
modals
    of ability and necessity, 152–153
    for speculating about the future, 152–153
    for speculating about the past, 124–125
negative questions, 96–97
nouns
    gerunds, 16–17, 40–41
    noun clauses, 140–141
reported speech, 68–69
tag questions, 108–109
verbs
    *be going to* and *will,* 146–157
    future events, 146–157
    future in the past, 128–129
    infinitives, 40–41
    *may/might/could,* 20–21, 112–113, 152–153
    *must,* 112–113
    passive voice, 28–29, 48–49
    passive voice with present progressive and present perfect tenses, 84–85
    past perfect tense, 33
    present perfect progressive tense, 4–5
    present perfect tense, 4–5
    *should have/could have/would have,* 136–137
    unreal conditional in the present, 56–57
    *wish* in the present, 60–61

## LISTENING

conversations, 5, 6, 9, 17, 21, 33, 45, 61, 65, 70, 73, 77, 85, 89, 90, 93, 101, 105, 115, 117, 127, 128, 129, 137, 149, 153
descriptions, 70
discussions, 6, 30, 90, 114
interviews, 150
presentations, 138, 152
radio programs, 18, 42, 58, 86, 110, 150

## PRONUNCIATION

*have/be* contractions, 7
intonation of finished vs. unfinished ideas, 127
intonation of tag questions, 110–111
intonation to show surprise, 91
linking words together, 31
past modals, 138–139
reduced *are,* 87
reduced speech: *d'ya* and *didja,* 58
reduction of *to,* 43

stress in compound nouns, 151
*th* sounds, 19
thought groups, 71

**READING SKILLS,** 10–11, 22–23, 34, 46–47, 62, 74, 90, 102, 118, 130, 154

## READINGS

*Music is Medicine, Music Is Sanity* 50–51
*Salvation (And Profit) In Greentech* 34–35
*Three Things I Learned While My Plane Crashed* 114–115
*Five Dangerous Things (You Should Let Your Children Do)* 142–143
*Hands Across Time,* 130–131
*The Hubble Space Telescope,* 154–155
*In Sports, Red Is the Winning Color,* 102–103
*In Your Face,* 22–23
*Pioneers of the Pacific,* 10–11
*The Rickshaws of Kolkata,* 90–91
*Saving a City's Public Art,* 74–75
*Survival School,* 62–63

## SPEAKING

asking and answering questions, 6–7, 9, 21, 31, 58, 100, 133, 141, 153
brainstorming, 59
class presentations, 151
conversations, 9, 17, 41, 45, 61, 65, 73, 77, 85, 89, 90, 93, 101, 109, 113, 117, 125, 129, 137, 149
describing, 9, 12, 19, 21, 23, 45, 61, 72, 73, 119
discussing, 5, 16, 17, 18, 20, 25, 29, 31, 32, 33, 46, 52, 56, 59, 62, 71, 70, 74, 76, 78, 79, 86, 87, 88, 93, 95, 101, 104, 109, 110, 111, 112, 113, 126, 136, 139, 140, 141, 150, 157
explaining, 7, 21, 59, 67, 79, 91, 132, 139
interviewing, 7, 111
opinions, 71, 89
quiz questions, 139
recommending, 93
reporting, 69
role playing, 40, 87, 93, 111, 145
speculating, 125, 153

## TEST-TAKING SKILLS

checking off answers, 34, 50, 78, 105, 118, 142, 150, 159
chronological order, 38, 39, 154, 157
circling answers, 18, 22, 46, 47, 50, 53, 58, 78, 80, 81, 97, 111, 118, 120, 121, 139, 145, 158, 160
completing charts, 5, 6, 47, 81, 92, 111, 121, 150
definitions, 4, 8, 16, 20, 28, 44, 56, 60, 68, 72, 84, 96, 100, 102, 105, 108, 124, 130, 136, 148, 157
filling in blanks, 8, 18, 49, 60, 61, 77, 86, 101, 128, 129, 151, 153
labeling pictures, 30, 46, 48, 79, 112, 119, 159

list making, 12, 25, 29, 31, 45, 47, 53, 61, 62, 64, 65, 74, 92, 93, 104, 117, 151, 156

matching, 8, 13, 16, 31, 34, 57, 70, 74, 80, 89, 109, 120, 142, 160

multiple choice, 37, 58, 98, 110, 126, 138, 139

ranking answers, 6, 30, 36, 93, 108, 114

sentence completion, 5, 8, 9, 13, 17, 20, 21, 25, 29, 31, 34, 37, 45, 57, 73, 78, 80, 85, 93, 101, 110, 113, 118, 125, 129, 133, 137, 158, 160

true or false, 18, 22, 38, 46, 50, 53, 65, 90, 102, 114, 117, 154

underlining answers, 31, 33, 65, 71, 113, 149, 153

## TOPICS

Art, 66–77

Changing Planet, 26–37

Competition, 94–104

Danger, 106–117

Getting Around, 82–93

Learning, 134–145

The Mind, 14–25

Money, 42–53

Mysteries, 122–133

People and Places, 2–13

Space, 146–157

Survival, 54–65

## VIDEO JOURNALS

*Andean Weavers,* 65

*Big City Bicycle Messengers,* 93

*Butler School,* 145

*Daring Mighty Things: Curiosity Lands on Mars,* 157

*Crop Circles,* 133

*Destroyers,* 117

*Making a Deal,* 53

*Memory Man,* 25

*The Netherlands: Rising Water,* 37

*Faces of India,* 77

*San Francisco's Mission District,* 13

*Women in the Rodeo,* 105

## VOCABULARY

art, 68, 72

climate, 8

dangers, 108, 112

education, 136, 140

emergencies, 108

environmental conservation, 60

large numbers, 32

mental processes, 16

migration, 4

money, 44

mysteries, 124

scientific studies, 20

space exploration, 148

sports, 96, 100

surprises, 128

survival, 56

transportation, 84, 88

## WRITING

advertising, 64

advice, 104

article, 116

bullet-point list, 104

composition, 156

description, 76, 132

personal experience, 24

letters, 92

news article, 36

opinions, 144

paragraphs, 12, 52, 76, 144, 156

## ILLUSTRATION

**18:** (m) Nesbitt Graphics, Inc.; **27:** (inset) Nesbitt Graphics, Inc.; **46:** (m) National Geographic Maps; **48:** (1, 2, 3, 4, 5, 6, 7) Nesbitt Graphics, Inc.; (8) Kenneth Batelman; **53:** (inset) Nesbitt Graphics, Inc.; **59:** (t) Ted Hammond/IllustrationOnline.com; **62, 65:** (inset) National Geographic Maps; **98:** (m) Nesbitt Graphics, Inc.; **100:** (b) Ted Hammond/IllustrationOnline.com; **110:** (b) National Geographic Maps; **112:** (1, 2, 3, 4, 5, 6) Ralph Voltz/IllustrationOnline.com; **129:** (t) Nesbitt Graphics, Inc.; **145:** (inset) National Geographic Maps.

## PHOTO

Cover Photo: Courtesy Manuel de la Higuera

**2–3:** (f) Dean Conger/National Geographic Creative; **4:** (tl) THOMAS J. ABERCROMBIE/National Geographic Creative; **5:** (r) Annie Griffiths Belt/National Geographic Creative; **6:** (t) FRANS LANTING/National Geographic Creative; **7:** (tr) TUYOSHI/Getty Images; **8:** (tl) Lynn Johnson/National Geographic Creative; **9:** (tr) FRANS LANTING/National Geographic Creative; **10–11:** (f) Stephen Alvarez/National Geographic Creative; **11:** (inset) TIM LAMAN/National Geographic Creative; **12:** (t) Douglas Peebles Photography/Alamy; **13:** (t) Mike Theiss/National Geographic Creative; (mr) Ty Milford/Getty Images; **14–15:** (f) © Graham McGeorge; **16:** (tl) PIERRE-PHILIPPE MARCOU/AFP/Getty Images; **18:** (tl) The Gallery Collection/Corbis; **19:** (t) MARK THIESSEN/National Geographic Creative; (mr) © iStock.com/pierredesvarre; (br) © Sandro Donda/Shutterstock.com; **20:** (tl) Martin Harvey/Corbis; **21:** (br) © Sigapo/Shutterstock.com; **22:** (f) CARY WOLINSKY/National Geographic Creative; **24:** (t) Stacy Gold/National Geographic Creative; **25:** (tl) © Sebastian Kaulitzki/Shutterstock.com; **26–27:** (f) James Balog/Aurora Photos; **28:** (tl) Mattias Klum/National Geographic Creative; **30:** (t) Daniel Loretto/iStock/360/Getty Images; (1) NASA GODDARD LABORATORY FOR ATMOSPHERIC SCIENCES SEVERE STORM BRANCH/National Geographic Creative; (2) LAIF/Redux; (3) NARINDER NANU/AFP/Getty Images; (4) Valentine/Getty Images; **31:** (mr) Corbis; **32:** (tl) Auscape/Universal Images Group/Getty Images; **33:** (br) George Grall/National Geographic Creative; **35:** (t) Robert Leslie/TED; **36:** Hans-Peter Merten/Stone/Getty images; **37:** (t) © Eric Gevaert/Shutterstock.com; **38:** PAUL NICKLEN/National Geaographic Creative; **39:** (t) TED; (bl, r, c, b) PAUL NICKLEN/National Geographic Creative; **41:** (t) PAUL NICKLEN/National Geographic Creative; **42–43:** (f) Crhister Fredriksson/Lonely Planet Images/Getty Images; **44:** (t) architecture UK/Alamy; **45:** (mr) Tim Graham/Getty Images; **46:** (m) Chris Hellier/Alamy; (t) O. LOUIS MAZZATENTA/National Geographic Creative; (tr) MPI/Stringer/Archive Photos/Getty Images; **49:** (tr) Hugh Sitton/Corbis; **50:** (t) James Duncan Davidson/TED; **51:** (l) Martin Scutt/dpa/Corbis; **53:** (t) Jean-Pierre Lescourret/Lonely Planet Images/Getty Images; **54–55:** (f) JASON EDWARDS/National Geographic Creative; **56:** (tl) Jason Persoff Stormdoctor/Corbis; **57:** (mr) Panamint Media/ Contributor/Moment Mobile/Getty Images; **58:** (tl) ESAM OMRAN AL-FETORI/Reuters/Corbis; **60:** (ml) BRIAN J. SKERRY/National Geographic Creative; **61:** (mr) Achim Mittler, Frankfurt am Main/Moment Select/Getty Images; **62–63:** (f) Jan Greune/LOOK/Getty Images; **62:** (bl) Paul Airs/Alamy; **64:** (t) Bean There/Getty Images; **65:** (t) Ralph Lee Hopkins/National Geographic Creative; **66–67:** (f) Kimberley Coole/Lonely Planet Images/Getty Images; **68:** (t) Diego Lezama/Lonely Planet Images/Getty Images; **69:** (br) George Ostertag/George Ostertag; **70:** (a) epa/Corbis; (b) Alfredo Dagli Orti/The Art Archive/Art Resource, NY; (c) Muskopf, Michael Todd/Muskopf, Michael Todd; (d) Eileen Tweedy/The Art Archive/Art Resource, NY; (e) Fine Art Photographic Library/Fine Art Photographic Library; **72:** (t) David Livingston/ Contributor/Getty Images Entertainment/Getty Images; **72–75:** (t) Kord.com/Age Fotostock; **76:** (t) Andrew Watson/John Warburton-Lee Photography/Alamy; **77:** (t) Steve McCurry/Magnum Photos; **78:** (tl) KEENPRESS/National Geographic Creative; **79:** (tr) James Duncan Davidson/TED; (1) Ron Levine/Digital Vision/Getty Images; (2) Leemage/Universal Images Group/Getty Images; (3, 4) TED; **80:** (tl) STAN HONDA/AFP/Getty Images; **81:** (tr) TAYLOR KENNEDY-SITKA PRODUCTIONS/National Geographic Creative; **82–83:** (f) © Shingo Morinaka/Prime 500px; **84:** (lc) RUBY WASHINGTON/The New York Times/Redux; **85:** (tr) Marco Grob/National Geographic Creative; (rm) © Visaro/Shutterstock.com; (rb) © Galyna Andrushko/Shutterstock.com; **86:** (t) © iStock.com/jorgeantonio; (inset) FRANS LANTING/National Geographic Creative; **87:** (tr) © wang song/Shutterstock.com; **88:** (t) Marion Kaplan/Alamy; **89:** (rm) Tom Bonaventure/Getty Images; **90–91:** (f) Saumalya Ghosh/FlickrVision/Getty Images; **92:** (t) Bob Henry/Alamy; **93:** (t) Bob Henry/Alamy; **94–95:** (f) © Dr. Wei Seng Chen; **96:** (tr) MOHAMMAD FAROOQ/AFP/Getty Images; **97:** (br) © iStock.com/technotr; **98:** (t) © iStock.com/proxyminder; **100:** (tl) Fuse/Getty Images; **101:** (rm) Andy Cross/Denver Post/Getty Images; **102–103:** KATE THOMPSON/National Geographic Creative; **103:** (tr) Cyril Ruoso/ Minden Pictures/Getty Images; **104:** (t) Rodolfo Molina/Euroleague Basketball/Getty Images; **105:** (t) Cultura Travel/Ben Pipe Photography/The Image Bank/Getty Images; **106–107:** (f) Mark Thiessen/National Geographic Creative; **108:** (tl) BRIAN J. SKERRY/National Geographic Creative; **109:** (rm) Tim Laman/National Geographic Creative; **110:** (tl) Joachim Hiltmann/imageBROKER/Alamy; (rm) CARY WOLINSKY/National Geographic Creative; **111:** (tr) Randy Wells/CORBIS; **115:** (t) James Duncan Davidson/TED; **116:** (l) Brendan McDermid/Reuters; **117:** (t) Roberto Caccuri/Contrasto/Redux; (tr) © iStock.com/slobo; (rm) © Shawn Talbot/Shutterstock.com; (rm) © iStock.com/stocknroll; (br) © Carsten Reisinger/Shutterstock.com; **118:** (t) Tom Pennington/Getty Images; **119:** (t) James Duncan Davidson/TED; (1) Jackson Lee/Splash News/Newscom; (2) James Duncan Davidson/TED; (3) Guven Demir/E+/Getty Images; (4) Steve Debenport/E+/Getty Images; **120:** (t) Doug Steley B/Alamy; **121:** (t) Alistair Berg/Iconica/Getty

## TEXT